A Fighter All My Life

THE LIFE AND WORDS OF

Sam Johnson

FROM ALABAMA TO LOS ANGELES TO DETROIT

ABECEDARIAN BOOKS · BALTIMORE, MARYLAND

A Fighter All My Life
Copyright ©2014 Sam Johnson

Front Cover Photo by: Madalyn Ruggiero
Cover Design by: Marc Christensen at Emdash Publishing (Canada)

Published by

Abecedarian Books, Inc.
2817 Forest Glen Drive
Baldwin, Maryland 21013-9574

Contents

Editor's Introduction

This is Sam Johnson's story, a man who was a fighter all his life, but who became aware of "the big picture," as he put it, and finally became a revolutionary militant, as many others did, during the 1970s.

These are oral reminiscences, from memory, not from notes or any diaries that Sam kept. Many things he forgot. Other things weren't important for him. But the events and impressions recorded here are what loomed large in the memory of one man who lived in Alabama under segregation and Jim Crow, then in Los Angeles and Detroit during the social rebellions of the 1960s and '70s.

Some dates and names could be checked via obituaries, on the internet, with other people or in the files he kept from union activity—but some could not be. The quotes obviously can only be approximations of what was said many decades ago, but they give the sense of what was going on. There undoubtedly are some inaccuracies. The book was done essentially from memory.

This book began as a series of conversations more than ten years ago, maybe longer, with Sam talking to several younger people about his life growing up in the South. It sat for awhile, but then it turned into a project. We began to tape the conversations, and follow his life up to the present. What had begun as a few evenings' conversations turned into ten tapes, over sixty minutes each. The last chapter was based on speeches and comments that Sam made at public meetings or the Spark festivals.

A friend, Larry Christensen, began to transcribe the tapes—a long and sometimes difficult task, given the equipment he had to work on.

The transcripts wandered a lot, as conversations do, jumping from one period to another, cycling back on the same incident many hours later.

Several years ago, I began to work with Sam to edit the transcripts: getting rid of duplications, getting him to explain something a little more, taking it down as he talked it through, reordering the material, and so on. But this is truly Sam's book, the account of an extraordinary life, a militant life, during the years of a very extraordinary period in American history.

Judith Carpenter

Sam Johnson's Introduction

MY WHOLE LIFE, I've been a fighter. Even before I was a teenager, I wouldn't accept that someone came messing with me. I was quiet. I didn't go looking for trouble. But I wouldn't just stand by and let someone get over on me.

When I got to be a teenager, I could see the racism. I saw the little white kids following in the same footsteps. They didn't understand what they were saying, but they saw it all around them and grew up learning to fall into the same racist ways their parents had.

By the time I was in my early teens, during the 1950s, the cops were already harassing me and my brother and my cousins. A lot of them were Ku Klux Klan and, being cops, they felt they could do what they wanted to the black kids. You knew if you did anything, they'd put you in jail. I was seventeen years old the first time they took me to jail, that time because of the 1956 curfew. I had just come from a teen dance, and I wasn't even on the street. I was in a little café and restaurant run by the family of my future sister-in-law. I was with my twenty-one-year-old cousin who was going to take me and my younger brother home. But I had my older brother's coat on, a U.S. Navy coat. He was home on leave. The cops wanted to know if it was my coat. One of them said, "You must be one of them smart ones that just got back."

Sometimes I thought about getting a shotgun and sprinkling them, but I understood, even back then, it wouldn't change anything.

Many of the older blacks were really afraid. They had seen all that lynching and the KKK right there in the police. But the way I grew up, I felt that if someone came after me, they might get me, but I thought I'd get somebody, too. That's just how I felt. I didn't have that fear.

I think I learned that from my mother because she was a fighter. She wasn't afraid of the cops. She was a strong person. A lot of men don't give women respect, but they gave my mother respect.

When I was twenty, my mother sent me, my brother Ocie and my cousin Carlos to Los Angeles so we wouldn't be killed by the cops. She knew what the cops were like and she knew that we wouldn't go along with the way they were treating black people, especially young black men.

My whole life I worked. Even before I was a teenager, I helped my mother, using a little wheelbarrow to carry the gallon jugs of corn liquor from a neighbor down the street when she ran out of her own stuff. Sometimes I helped clean up and take things to the garbage dump for the Italian man who ran the neighborhood grocery. When I was eleven, I started helping my cousins and my oldest brother on the carts they pushed around for an ice cream company. By the time I was twelve, I was pushing my own cart, and by fourteen, I was riding a bike that had a big cart on the front of it. When I dropped out of high school, I went to work in the plant where they made the ice cream in Bessemer, Alabama. I had just turned sixteen. When I went to L.A., I got a job at the carwash, then I worked as a janitor for a contractor in different buildings, then as a painter for Northrop Aircraft. After I moved to Detroit, I worked as a machine operator in a small parts plant, then as a die setter in the same plant. Then I went to Chrysler, where I worked for thirty years on the assembly line at different plants until I retired in 1999.

In Los Angeles, I started talking to some of the Black Muslims because they talked about things other people didn't. From the time I came to Detroit in 1967, I was interested in knowing more about the system, and where I fit in. I ran into some Black Muslims and started to read Muhammad Speaks, the newspaper of the Nation of Islam. But eventually I came to realize there was a bigger picture than what the Muslims saw. Malcolm X had begun to see that there was a system beyond what the Nation of Islam talked about, and I began to see that, too.

But I was hanging out, too, at different bars. I was running with the fast crowd, street people. I was hanging with all these people doing drugs and different things, and I was doing some of that, pills, smoking weed. I was hanging out, partying. And I was fighting, sometimes against people I knew.

In 1970, when I went to work at Dodge Main, I came in contact with some communists and I began to talk to them, and I got a bigger picture, looking at things from the viewpoint of the working class. With all the different problems I went through, I had a feeling I wanted to do something about it. But people always said, there's nothing you can do. But when I came in contact with the communists, I learned what the working class had done, I learned about the revolutions workers had made. And I began to realize that workers could make a revolution here in the U.S., and that things would only get worse until we did that.

From that day up until today, I have been active as a union militant and a revolutionary militant in the working class, trying to get other workers to see and understand what needs to be done, trying to bring workers to stand together to use the force they have. And I always tried to give them the bigger picture, where we fit in, to get them to understand how things could change if working people stood together, what we could do to defend ourselves and to build a different society.

July 2013

Part One
Alabama, 1939-59

One
My Family

MY MOTHER, SADIE B. WARE, was born in the year 1917 in Gainesville, Alabama, into a family of fourteen children, nine girls and five boys. Her mother and father were farmers in Sumpter County. She spent twenty years of her life on the farm, before she left and moved with my father and my two older brothers to Bessemer, which was about a hundred and some miles northeast of Gainesville.

My mother worked until she was fifty-three or so. She worked in the chicken house, cutting up chickens. She worked at a dry cleaners and laundry. And she worked cleaning houses and schools. And when she wasn't working, she had parties on Friday and Saturday. I can remember, even before she came out on disability, she had week-end parties and sold corn liquor, Moonshine, they called it. A lot of Alabama people had other names for the liquor, like Joe Louis. She sold that Moonshine as long as I can remember. She made double just on Friday and Saturday what the highest-paid workers at Pullman were making in a week. When a crowd come over on the week-ends, they'd be spending money for fish sandwiches and other food. Some of the cousins would be running a dice game, shooting dice, or playing some kind of card game, and she was getting a cut out of that. She sold fish and hot dogs and liquor. Somebody else was making it, but she'd buy a gallon, couple of gallons, then sell it, by

3

the shot glass or half a pint. Every time she sold half a pint, that was a dollar. Most people were going to get half a pint. That's where most of the money came from.

All those years she sold Moonshine and never was busted. Somebody sent the cops to the house, saying she was selling liquor there, but they never did find it. I remember she had two places under the floor of the house on 10th Avenue, one in the bedroom, and one under the floor in the bathroom. Put it under the floor and then put a rug on top of it. When she got ready to get some, she would just move that rug out of the way, pull up a couple of those boards and get the liquor out, then cover it back up.

In the new house down in Jonesboro, she had a hiding place in a little heater. It had a hole in the back of it, and she used to pour all of the liquor into bottles, mostly half pint, and then stick them in the back of the heater. If the heater isn't burning, there's nothing in the heater, maybe some burnt wood. But she had her liquor in the back of it, in that hole. They didn't think about looking there for that liquor. They'd look all up in the closet, under the beds, in the chifferobe, in the trunk, everywhere. Ain't found no liquor yet. That's where she used to hide it—in a heater, a wood and coal heater.

That's when they told her, "Sadie, if you got that liquor, you is a better hider than we is a finder."

My mother said, "I told you there weren't no liquor in here. Maybe you should go search the place of who sent you over here. Maybe you'll find your liquor."

Sadie B. was a person who could not read, not even at a second or third grade level, but she could handle some money.

And she wasn't afraid. My mother was real tough. My daddy was a big man, but when she and my daddy got into it, anything she could get in her hands, she would come at him with it. If he turned loose of her for a minute, she would get something and she'd be coming at him. Most times he didn't want to have a fight with her because he'd be wanting to stop and he couldn't stop her. Every time she'd get her hands on something she'd be coming to blast him with it. So then he would hold her and say "All right, Sadie, all right," because if he let her go, she would just go and get something else and come right back at him. That was the way she was. So he didn't want no fight with her because she would take it further than he wanted to go with it.

Normally a man would just beat the woman up and that's it. No. Not with Sadie B. If you don't watch it, YOU are going to get beat up. That's the way she was. I saw that when I was growing up.

One time, in the 1950s, she was over to her sister Clara Mae's house where they were having a little party. Clara Mae's husband Strode was beating her, knocking her from one side of the room to the other, just beating her. Everybody was scared to mess with Strode. He was big.

My mother came in there. And she called him two times, "Jake!" His name was Strode, but they called him Jake. "Jake! Jake!" He seemed like he didn't hear her.

She picked up this doggone pop bottle and just crowned him right across the forehead, right across the temple, POW, with that bottle. Blood was coming out on his face. Right away, that stopped him right there.

"OK Sadie. OK Sadie. OK Sadie."

Everybody else was scared, afraid to get into it, but she stopped him with that bottle.

She had some history. One of my cousins accused my mother of dating her man, having a relationship with him. It was a lie, and my mother went to check her out. Some of my cousin's folks were at her house. When they saw Sadie B. coming, they tried to hold the door closed. But my mother just busted in the door, went in there and beat the cousin up. She wouldn't let someone tell a lie on her.

5

Sadie B. really was one of the nicest persons there ever was, but she wasn't taking no shit from nobody, police, nobody. She would say what she had to say. That's where I got a lot of that from, from my mother.

Sam's Grandfather, William Ware, and his mother, Sadie B. Ware Johnson

Ma'Dear, that's what we grew up calling her, although when we grew older sometimes we called her Sadie B., like everyone else did.

She looked out for the family and others as long as I can remember. Almost all the time, we had extra people in the house. Most of the cousins in the family and friends of the family who came from Gainesville stayed with us. Time one of them got out of the house, there'd be somebody else. They'd be already set to come, then Ma'Dear would let them know when to come. They were leaving Gainesville, and she was the person who got them started. This went on all the time. When they came to Bessemer, they didn't have nowhere to go. Most of them didn't have any other relatives there, no money. So my mother let them stay until they got themselves a little job, and then they'd be gone. Time they get out of the house, boom, here's another one.

It was like the history of that time. They were leaving the farm and coming to Bessemer. It's a big city when you're leaving the farm and coming to Bessemer. They called it the Little Pittsburgh of the South, because it had heavy industry, built steel pipes, built trains, bridges. All this production went on in Bessemer. TCI was six, seven miles away—that's where they built all the steel for bridges and big construction.

So they came to Bessemer. Ma'Dear gave them a place to stay until they got a little job and they could get them a place and go on out. She was almost like something I read in a book about Harriet Tubman, when she brought the slaves up, one trip after another. She had connections, and she brought them up.

This went on all the time in the house, people coming and going. I don't know how it looked. There were two big rooms, plus the kitchen. We had four beds. We had a bed, plus one of those couch beds, not a full size bed, in the front room, plus a dresser. In the other room there was a big old heater—about five feet tall, one of them big heaters with a big pot in the center. This heater was sitting in there against the wall; then there was a bed here and one next to it, and a little one over there, and a shelf where you could put something in back of the heater. I can't understand how a room had that much in it. Then we had a chifferobe—one of those pieces of furniture you hang clothes in, and it had drawers. That was sitting right at the foot of the bed on the right. All this in that one room.

Sometimes there was an organ in the room, too, that my daddy played.

In the front room, there was also a big TV. My mother bought one of the first big TVs that anyone had around Bessemer, a 25-inch that sat on the floor. We loved to have that 25-inch screen and all us kids sitting back on the floor like we were in the movies.

Then we moved down to Jonesboro. My daddy bought a house down there, and they remodeled it, shaped it up the way they wanted it. We moved down there in 1956. It was bigger and it had three bedrooms. After my daddy died, Ma'Dear had people come in and expand the porch and build a little sitting room and another bathroom.

MY FATHER, SAM JOHNSON JR., was born in 1917 in Gainesville, Alabama, into a family of five, three girls and two boys. My father's mother and father were also farmers who lived in Gainesville, Sumpter County. He spent about nineteen or twenty years of his life on that farm before he left and moved to Bessemer with my mother and my two older brothers, Willie and Jesse.

My daddy worked different jobs, in the beginning in the coal mines. Later on, he was hired into one of the biggest industries in the South, Pullman, where they built freight cars for carrying cargo. He put the big wheels on the freight cars. Once I was headed home from school, and he was walking home from Pullman, got out of work early. We just connected and walked home together. He liked to play the organ and he played the guitar.

My father was a person who spent half of his time with other women, and he had at least three other kids with other women. We had two half sisters and a brother, younger than us, and we knew them.

My daddy was one of those men who believed in controlling their women. But from what I can remember, it didn't work out so well with my mother, Sadie B. One time, my mother hid in the back seat of his car. This was sometime in the 1940s. I was eight or nine, somewhere. She knew my daddy was messing around, so she wanted to see where he was going. She got in the car before he took off. When he got in the car, she was already there. He went over to one of his women's house, and he had no idea my mother was in the car. No idea that she was lying down on the floor of the car in the back seat.

The woman came out by the car. I think she saw my mother move, and she said to my daddy, "Who's that, who's in the back?"

"Ain't nobody in there, woman, get in the car."

About that time my mother said she just got up and came out and grabbed the woman and beat her up.

Sam Johnson, Jr., Sam's father

MY FATHER'S SISTER, Aunt Ella Jane, used to have fish fries and parties on the week-end at her house in Pipe Shop, like my mother did. My auntie had this jukesbox, that's what they called it, where you could put money in to play music. When I was nine or ten, the KKK came through one night and told her, "You're gonna stop these parties and take that jukesbox out of the house."

My auntie told them right away she was not taking the jukesbox out.

"When we come back you better have it out."

She said, "Well, come on back. I'm not taking my jukesbox out of my house. This box ain't going nowhere."

The KKK burned a cross in front of her house. They said they were coming back, and they set a date to come back. She told the family and her friends about it. My family got together, and friends of my family got together. They had a hundred and some people out there on that date, waiting on the KKK. It would have been something, it really would have been history if the KKK had shown up. Waiting on the KKK, they all had their rifles and shotguns and pistols. They were all in the grass, ringed around a two-block, three-block area. The KKK would have been surrounded if they'd come back up in there. All those people were in the grass where the KKK couldn't see them, wouldn't know they were there.

I know my father, he was like a lot of black men in that time period, he was afraid of the cops and of what white people could do to his family. But he was ready to throw down. This was his sister. So he was down there with his gun. The family was prepared, waiting on them, waiting on them to come back. People were mad anyway. This was in the late 1940s.

The KKK didn't show. And they never did come back. They probably got the message. A black person could have informed the cops, and the cops would have told the KKK. If it was a black person who told the cops, they probably knew my family and knew they would fight.

My daddy died young, only forty-one, cancer of the throat that spread. He didn't really smoke that much, or drink that much, but his jobs had a lot of pollution where he worked.

My mother lived forty-one years longer than he did. She passed at eighty-two.

Two
Daily Life in Bessemer

I WAS BORN 1939 in Gainesville, Alabama, my mother's third child. She went back to the farm to have me. My father's mother was one of those midwives who brought children into the world. There weren't hardly any doctors for black women then.

Ma'Dear went back to the farm to have my younger brother Ocie, too. But I don't remember it. He was two years and three months behind me.

The first thing I can remember, I was three years old in Bessemer, watching my oldest brother Willie and my big cousins putting a bag over their heads. They tore holes out so they could see. But I didn't, I just grabbed a bag and put it over my head and then ran out in the road and sat down.

They called it "road" then because they hadn't even paved the street that ran in front of the house. When you're in the road, you're on dirt, just like the dirt in the yard. I didn't realize I was in the street. I was three years old, couldn't see and had the bag on my head, down over my whole body—a cleaner's bag. At that time they were putting paper bags over the clothes, just a regular brown paper sack.

A guy driving a truck had started to run right over the bag thinking there was nothing in it. But when he saw the bag move, he knew something was in it, and he stopped his truck. That's what he told my mother when my mother came out.

This was in Bessemer, 10th Avenue between 18th and 19th Streets. We lived in a brick house there, one of two brick houses on that street, ours and the one next door. At that time period, even in Bessemer, most of the people didn't have inside toilets. They had outside toilets, outhouses. We did have an inside toilet, but we had to go out of the back door and then go through a door on the porch to go into the bathroom.

Most of the whole city had outdoor toilets. In the areas where the whites lived, I think most of those houses had indoor toilets. A lot of them were middle class.

You had one area would be black, go right up to this street here, and then it stopped. And after that it was all white up that way. Big houses were down through there, so I know it had to be middle class because the poor working class whites couldn't afford those big houses.

There were a few small houses where some of the whites lived, but most of the working class whites lived out of the city on the outskirts of the city. They didn't live right in Bessemer. The ones who lived in the city had to be middle class. I checked that out later when I went back down there, looking at those big houses where they stayed. Couldn't have been poor whites in those houses, they're too big.

ONE DAY, I WAS downtown shopping with my mother, and we were in the 5 and 10 Cent Store. They had signs on the water fountain saying "White Only." Ma'Dear told me that I couldn't drink the water out of it. But when she went around to the other side of the store, I went up to the water fountain and drank some of that water. I had to drink this water because I wanted to know what white people's water tasted like. I wasn't any more than five years old at the time.

A GUY CAME BY the house one day. I was maybe five or six. We were all out in the yard playing, and one of my cousins, Rob, saw him and said something to him, just playing. The guy threw his knife, this dirk, and it stuck right in the wood post holding up the porch. Boom.

My mother was standing in the door and said "What's wrong with you, you crazy? You could have hurt one of those kids throwing that knife."

The guy said, "Oh, I was just playing, I wasn't trying to hurt nobody."

But the next year, he killed Joseph, one of my older cousins, with a knife. My cousin was at a party, and he got into a fight with that same guy. The guy stabbed Joseph in the neck, and my cousin died the next day. Stabbed him, the blade went right through his hat, hit an artery.

The next day, I went down to the house where it happened. I was no more than six or seven at the time. I got my cousin's hat, it was still lying out there in front of the house. It had a hole in it where he was stabbed, and I wore the hat back to our house.

It wasn't the idea that it had a hole in it, just that it was his hat. I knew all these cousins. They had all stayed at our house before, when they first came to Bessemer. The one who was killed did. His brother did. Most all of them when they first came, they stayed at our house.

That's all I knew. I was a kid, I got the hat and wore it back to the house. My mother just took the hat off. I think that was it.

THEY USED TO HAVE Christmas parades downtown for the kids. I remember one time when I was about six or seven, Santa was riding down the street throwing candies out to the kids. This white woman said to a little white kid, "Don't let HIM get the candy," pointing to me. Like Santa's candy wasn't for black kids.

THOMAS DEW, Daddy's brother, got into it with some guys. They were messing with him, so he shot at them. Then the guys called the cops. He gave his wife Mamie the gun, and she ran down to our house with the gun. When she came in there, she gave it to my mother. My mother was in the bed. She took the gun and put it right up under her. She was sitting on the side of the bed, sitting on the gun.

By the time my Aunt Mamie got there, the cops were banging on the door, Boom, Boom, Boom. They said they saw her running. Anyway they kept yelling, "Where that gun at?"

Mamie said, "I ain't got no gun."

Police said, "Your husband said you have it."

Auntie was looking scared. I guess she was about ready to tell them she gave it to my mother. Ma'Dear gave her that hard look, like "you better NOT say nothing." Sadie B. wasn't afraid of the police.

One of the cops grabbed the end of the bed and started to look under the mattress. Ma'Dear never moved off the bed. They didn't know Mamie brought the gun in the house, they just assumed it. She could have thrown it somewhere. But police were coming in the house anyway, going to search under the bed.

But my Uncle Carlos cut that cop off. Uncle Carlos, married to one of my mother's sisters, was there and he was a talker too. He had been in New York or Akron, Ohio, one of those two, but came back. When people live up North, they have a different attitude when they come back to the South. When this cop did that, Uncle Carlos said right out, "What are you doing? Don't you see this woman is in her bed?"

So the cop put the mattress back down. The cops were white, nothing but white cops in the South then. They finally gave up on that one. I was about five or six, watching all that.

ONE OF MY MOTHER'S half-brothers was at home. He was in World War II, and he said he wasn't going back to that war, so he went AWOL. The MP's were looking for him, came to our house. Had some kind of stool pigeon with them, a black guy, bringing them to where the family lived. He brought them to our house and some of the other houses. They were asking questions, "Where is he?" Ma'Dear looked right at them. "He left here. I don't know where he went." She wasn't going to tell them no way. Finally, he turned himself back in. They gave him a dishonorable discharge. I heard him in the house, talking, "I ain't going back in that war."

My uncles were in the army in that war. I can remember, they came to our house and talked about it. They said the army didn't put too many guns in black soldiers' hands. The government was afraid of what could happen.

ANOTHER YOUNG BLACK guy in that war was home on leave. About two blocks from where we lived, a cop got into it with him. The cop said something nasty to him, then pulled out his gun. A lot of black men went in that war, risked their lives, but then came back and the white cops messed with them. It's just like they were back in the war.

The soldier pulled some judo on him—they called it jiu-jitsu—flipped him and grabbed the gun, Boom, killed the cop right there. The cop had his little boy, eight or nine years old, right there with him, in the car with him. That little boy saw his daddy get killed.

That little boy came to be a cop as soon as he got old enough. He patrolled right there where we lived. It was the same area where his father was killed. Oh, did he fuck with black people! He was a monster. He had this idea in his mind, "A black man killed my daddy." He took it out on all black people. He was crazier than his daddy.

Three
Growing Up Learning to Fight

I WAS MOVED AROUND a lot in school. The schools for the black kids were crowded, and we were ripped around from place to place. When I started elementary school, I was sent over to Dunbar High, which was about a mile from my house. At that time, the junior high and high school were all in the same building, and the grade school was in the building put up next to it. I went to Dunbar for two years or something like that. Then they transferred us out of there because they said we were out of the district, so I was sent to Carver Junior High for grade school. It was in Jonesboro, further away. They had started building 22nd Street Elementary, about four blocks from my house. When I started back up in the fall, I went to 22nd Street up to the sixth grade. Then, I went back to Dunbar for junior high.

AT CARVER, when I was eight or nine, I had a fight with this guy. I found out later he was in my family on my daddy's side, but I didn't know that then. He didn't know it either. I was leaning back in my chair in the classroom, when he pushed the chair and I fell back and hit my head on the floor. Put a knot on my head.

When I got out, I told my older brother Willie about it. He told me, "Well, hit him then."

So I jumped this guy and was hitting him, but then his

18

brother Joseph tried to get into it—ran up there, going to try to get me.

My cousin James Ware snatched him back and said "No, hold it, it ain't your turn yet." He pulled him back, just like that, and I was OK after that.

I had another fight out on the playground at Carver. This bully started to grab me. He thought he could deal with me, he was much bigger than me. When he grabbed me, I just started wrestling and tussling with him. Threw his big ass on the ground and was down on him.

MY OLDER BROTHERS and cousins taught me how you hold somebody down. If you got him down, you lay crossways over him so he can't get up. If he turns this way or that other way, either way you can use your weight, push your weight this way or pull your weight that way, keep him down. If he tries to flip you over, you still got more ground to hold back. He can't just throw you on over. But if you are just on top of him, straight, a bigger person can flip you over just like that. They got the weight. If I had just tossed him down, he would have tossed me off him.

Once I saw my daddy and our next door neighbor tussling in the house, just wrestling. My daddy was two hundred thirty or two-forty, but the neighbor flipped him. But the neighbor didn't hold him right. The minute my daddy hit the floor, he threw this guy off him, and put all his weight on the guy.

I had to wrestle with bigger people, so I learned how to hold them down. Running, wrestling, boxing, at an early age, I was running with the bigger kids, my brothers and my older cousins. My age group couldn't touch me. It was just like somebody was working out and training like a fighter. Most kids didn't do that, but I was swimming with older kids, running with them, biking with them. I was riding with the big boys and staying right with them. I didn't care how fast they go. You learn how to do that. Biking and running, you stay right with them because you can't get left.

Sometimes my brothers didn't want to be bothered looking out for me. Willie was almost four years older than me, and Jesse was two years older. When they went with the big boys, friends of theirs, three or four years older than me, they didn't want me with them.

But I'd be determined to go. "I ain't going back."

So one of them would hit me, telling me to go back. Then they would take off running. Shit, I would stay right with them. Then they stop, I stop. If they come back, I run back the other way because they're still mad. I run back, but when they stop, I stop. They turn around and run away again, I run right with them. When I wanted to go, I was going. "I ain't going back home. I want to go with y'all."

I HAD ONE FIGHT when I was sent to Carver Junior High for grade school. I was coming home, and three guys jumped on me, beat me up. Later on, one of them came walking up on 18th Street, right by where my family lived. So I went out there and got him. I boxed his head. We called him Joe Louis, but I was the Joe Louis that time. I think he was a little older than me, but he went home crying.

When I got to this elementary school on 22nd Street, I had a lot of fights. There was one guy who was always a bully. He just picked with me. He didn't need to be messing with me. But that's how he was. He just kept pushing at me. So we got into it, and I whipped his butt. He was surprised and shocked because he really was a bully and I whipped his ass.

There was another guy at the 22nd Street school, who thought he was tough. He was steady messing with me in school. I told him, "You wait till we get out of school." I'd been fighting in school before, and I was trying not to get into something again in the school. He was about a year older than me. When we got out of school, we were walking back home when we got into it. His youngest brother, who was about a year younger than me, came behind me, punching me in the back. I turned around real quick and hit him a couple of times and he stopped. I got back on his big brother again. Boom, Boom, Boom.

Some of the neighbors came up and said, "Y'all stop that, now." So we stopped.

I never in my life just provoked and messed with someone else like bullies do. I never did that. But when they come on me, then I go to the max and kick their butts.

Only one guy I couldn't keep up with. He came from New York, I think. This guy had been boxing, training. I had a fight with him. He punched me down. And he was laughing. Pissed me off, but I couldn't get him back. The only one in those days.

Four
A Boy's Life

IN BESSEMER, there was a storage area with warehouses between 7th and 8th Avenues. There were rails running off where they dropped the trains to store them. The warehouse may be already loaded up, so they would stash the trains down there, then the next day or so bring them up to the warehouse and unload them. These boys that lived on 20th Street used to go over there, break into the box cars and take stuff out. The cars didn't have any locks on them; all they had was a little tin-wire hook holding it closed. Those boys just popped that little wire, broke it right off. They would steal stuff out of there—all kinds of stuff, boxes of stuff they would take out of there. Some of the houses were right there on 20th Street, and the front ends were sitting up on posts three or four feet from the ground. We used to play under the houses. But these older boys stacked the stuff they took under the houses until they sold it or got rid of it.

We used to play on the trains. Climb up on the trains when they were sitting there. Hang out down there. Shouldn't be down there, but we did it.

There was a bridge over the trains on 9th Avenue that went from 19th to 22nd Street. We used to sit down there on the bridge, down there on the corner of 19th Street and 9th Avenue. Sometimes, these older white guys would come by, mess with us. We were just sitting there watching cars come by. But they would come by there driving, say something nasty, throw cans or bottles at us. We decided, we'd get them. When they came by we had some bricks to throw back at them. So they took off. They were gone. After that, we didn't have any problem with them.

We were some bad kids. I guess that's why those farmers down in Gainesville would say to my grandma, "Lang, how you deal with them bad boys every year?" We were so much different from the people down on the farm. Had to be— we're in the city.

The sawmill was right there, too, off of 20th Street. Some of the Italian kids used to come down there, and we would all play together down there. In the afternoon, when the sawmill would close down, we'd all be up in there. We'd go on top of it, run down, get to the end of the roof, flip and land in a big pile of sawdust left over from cutting the wood. The sawdust wasn't that high, so you just do a flip and land on your feet, like you do off a diving board. We used to do that all the time.

WE USED TO SWIM at Tuxedo Park, which was in Ensley in the Birmingham district, about eight or nine miles away from Bessemer. I was a kid, I guess about seven or eight, and we had to take the bus over there. The pool there was the only one around that we could swim in at that time.

There was a pool nearby in Bessemer—it had been there for years, but it wasn't for blacks. It was one mile away from us, supposed to be public, our taxes paid on it, but it was only for whites. Up into the 1950s, it still was like that. Then in the '50s, protests against discrimination began. Rosa Parks in Montgomery—we heard she refused to give up her seat. After the big march in 1963, and then when the riots jumped off in Birmingham and Harlem, they started integrating some places. The Bessemer pool was integrated, maybe in 1964 or '65. But they shut the pool down once they integrated it.

They said the whites refused to swim with the blacks, and I guess they decided they weren't going to keep it going just for blacks. All these years it had been just a white pool, black taxes paid for it, and blacks couldn't swim in it. Now when whites refused to swim in it with blacks, they just shut the pool down. That's what they did.

We used to go swimming in every little swimming area around there. One time we were at West Lake, a little lake on the west side of Bessemer. My brother Jesse and his friend Sammy Lee were there. Sammy Lee couldn't swim. A lot of times, you look at water, you can see the bottom, and it doesn't look that deep. Sammy Lee was just messing around. He knew he couldn't swim, but he didn't think the water was over his head. He jumped in and thought he was going to stand up. But the water came over his head. It was deeper than he thought it was. He came up, his eyes bugging, and then he went down again. So then we knew he couldn't swim.

My cousin James Ware hollered, "Jesse, you better get that boy, Jesse."

Jesse was the best swimmer of the bunch. Jesse came in behind Sammy Lee, and when he came up the second time Jesse grabbed around him from the back and just pushed him to the shallow water. Then they stood up and walked on out.

One time we were at West Lake, and one kid had a gun. I thought it was a play gun, a cap pistol. We were skipping school. He brought this gun from home—maybe his brother or somebody had got it somewhere. He brought it down with him to West Lake, a .32 or something like that. He let me see it, and I took it and pointed it at him. Then I saw him dodging and going on, I knew something was wrong. "Man, this gun is real."

TWO WHITE GUYS came along. They were grown, one in his late thirties, one in his twenties, and they had been drinking too. We were at West Lake, in the lake with a friend we called Little Studie. They took Little Studie's bike and acted like they weren't going to give it back to him. We went behind them, thinking maybe they would give him his bike back. We got to the other end of the lake, where you come up on the road.

Little Studie was crying, saying, "Y'all give me my bike."

A middle-aged white guy lived right across from where we came up. He came over to see what was going on, and he asked us what was wrong.

Little Studie told him, "They done took my bike and won't give it back."

The guy came down with us, asked them, "What you guys doing? You got this boy's bike?"

"Well yeah, we was just playing with him."

"Well give him his bike."

They didn't much challenge him, didn't argue with him at all. He was white, he was living in a big house, they probably knew who he was.

"We was just playing with him, we wasn't going to do nothing, we wasn't going to take it." That's what they said—and gave Little Studie his bike back just like that.

And we just left.

SOMETIMES WE SWAM in the creek with no clothes on, got no swim trunks. We'd just swim naked back there in the little branch that went down beside West Lake. One day, we were there and this older guy, a black teenager, was swimming there naked. These white guys came down there with some white girls and got right in the branch. The black dude in the branch was telling us, "Hey, I need some swimming trunks." He had got real afraid, scared, thinking he was out there naked and those white girls were there. If somebody see him out there, they may come and do something to him. Those girls were laughing and carrying

25

on because they knew he was scared to come out. One of the guys who was there with him got out of the water and changed, then finally threw those swimming trunks out to him so he could get out. That was all West Lake stuff.

WE WENT FISHING at West Lake. We weren't supposed to be fishing there. But we did. One time, it was my brother Ocie and John Dew, a cousin, and Carlos, another cousin, and another young boy and me. Carlos and the others must have been about ten at the time, and I must have been about twelve. The cops came, and I took off into the swamp, Carlos and the young boy came right behind me. The cops followed us, but we got away. Ocie and John Dew got busted. But we went back later the same day and got our fishing rods and hooks and the fishes we caught.

MY BROTHER JESSE saved someone another time, at Three-Way. That was another creek we would swim in. We had a Two-Way and we had a Three-Way. I don't know why they named them like that. Most of the people just knew them by those names.

We had to come a pretty good piece to get there from where we lived. We were there with a guy named Willie Terry who lived down the street from us. He had the illusion that the water wasn't that deep. Certain areas of certain creeks, the water wouldn't be that deep, but it was eight feet or more there. But he didn't know that, plus he saw me swimming out there with my head up out of the water, and he thought I was standing on the bottom.

I went to dive and he told me, "I'm coming right behind you, man."

Here comes this fool, he didn't know how to really dive, here he comes Rrrr, Pow! And we just cracked up. Then he went down and was going to stand up, but he couldn't touch bottom. Then he came back up, scared, and he went back down again.

I think my cousin, James Ware, hollered for Jesse because if anyone could get him it would be Jesse.

Jesse came up to get him. The minute he came near Willie Terry, Willie grabbed Jesse, man, just locked on to him. Then they both went down. Then they came back up. They went down again. Jesse said he couldn't get loose from him. But one thing hit Jesse's mind, "This fool is steady trying to get to the top, well, take him down then." Jesse figured Willie would turn him loose if he stayed down. Just take him down and don't come back up with him. Jesse stayed down, and Willie came up. Then Jesse came right up behind him and grabbed him from the back. Pulled him to the shallow water. Got him. But both of them would have drowned if Jesse hadn't been thinking clear.

We also went swimming at Cement Bottom. It was another place like a branch, but for some reason, they had cemented it, concrete on the bottom, to take the water somewhere. That's why we named it Cement Bottom.

Then there was Blue Lake, right there on 9th Avenue Superhighway. Blue Lake wasn't that far from the house, about a mile. We used to go over there and swim a lot of times. It wasn't very big, more like a pond, but it was deep. Some people used to talk about it, they thought it had a "suck-hole" in it. Go too deep, and it would suck you in. But it was pretty good to swim in.

THEY BUILT A SKATING RINK right down the street from Blue Lake, an outdoor one, the first one in Bessemer where blacks could skate. They rented you the skates, roller skates, and you skated around. We had some good skaters used to come through there. We would skate quite a while, start in the evening time or late afternoon. I was eleven or twelve then.

We'd been skating on the streets and sidewalks for

five or six years already. So I was already pretty good at skating when they opened the rink. We'd skate to Brighton in Birmingham, and to Jonesboro in Bessemer. Some places in Bessemer we didn't skate. They didn't have sidewalks in some areas once you got out of the main city. Then some of the streets were messed up. Other streets were so busy, the cops would bust us for skating on them. But we skated on 18th Street all the time. That was a main street right near where I lived. That was our thing, skate on 18th Street—especially around Christmas and other holidays. We would skate on 18th Street from 9th Avenue to 12th Avenue. But we used to be a little careful near 9th Avenue. It was so busy because it was the main strip that comes through Bessemer. Superhighway, they called it—not that many lanes, but a lot of traffic.

Most of the time we would stop when we got to Joe Gardenia's store on 18th Street. We would still be half a block from 9th Avenue. If we got up there close to 9th Avenue, where cars were coming onto 18th Street, we'd be getting into more of a risk. The cars would be coming fast around the corner. We'd cut it off by 9th Alley. Then we would skate back down toward 12th Avenue—two and a half blocks we would skate on. Once in a while we may have gone across 9th Avenue, but we didn't make it our regular thing. Once we got across 9th Avenue, whites lived there, poor white, or Jewish who owned the stores in that neighborhood.

We used to do different things, skating backward, racing each other, skating long distance, growing up on those old iron-wheel skates, with the frames made of steel.

We went to different areas, skating sidewalks. A bunch of us, getting together, we would skate over to Brighton, northwest of Bessemer, or skate over to Jonesboro, south of Bessemer, and Mobile Junction, a couple miles south of Jonesboro. But to get to some areas like Brighton, we had to skate streets, on some parts they call highways, the hot little roads. We'd get in some areas before we got to Brighton where there weren't any houses and no sidewalks.

Brewerfield was where a lot of my aunties, my mother's sisters, and their kids lived. It was a hard place to skate to. It wasn't even in Birmingham district at that time, but Birmingham finally came further south and took over that area, along with Roosevelt. The cars were going forty miles an hour. And we got arrested if the cops saw us skating out there. But on the side of the road, we could ride our bikes. The best way was to go Superhighway up to Brewerfield. So we rode our bikes to go up there, go hang out with the cousins and aunties.

Some of my family on my daddy's side lived in Pipe Shop, in the Pipe Shop area. There was a big pipe shop for U.S. Pipe there, so they named the area after it. That was in Bessemer, down about 16th or 17th Avenue, you are in Pipe Shop. They made different kinds of pipe, all sizes, steel pipes and things. I had an uncle worked down there, and my brother Ocie worked there later on.

MY BROTHER OCIE was the baby boy, right behind me, two years younger than me. He was a kid who acted like they say the baby one acts—he's got to have everything. And he was a con artist at a very early age. When Ocie was six or seven, he used to steal people's empty milk bottles off their back porch. People set the bottles out for how much milk they wanted, and the milkman would take the empty bottles and leave new bottles of milk, then come back on the weekend to collect what people would be owing. Ocie used to go early in the morning before the milkman got there, and he'd get the bottles, take them to the store and get two cents for a bottle. And he used to steal people's dogs and try to sell them. The family had a joke about one of those mangy run-down dogs that Ocie stole. The dog was in such bad shape, Ocie had to prop it up when he went to sell it because the dog couldn't hardly stand!

Ocie used to be something else. Once, when I came home, I left my bike right out front, and I told Ocie, "Look man, I'm coming right back out, don't mess with my bike 'cause I'm coming right back out." I got in the house, tried to grab something to eat. When I came back out there, he had got the bike and gone with it, just like that.

I saw him coming down the street with it. So I grabbed a rock and threw it at him. I was just trying to scare him. I threw it in front of him, thought I was going to miss him, but by him coming toward me, that rock hit him right on his hand on the bar. Cut his hand, busted his hand.

He came in hollering, showed his hand to Daddy so he could see it. Crying, blood was coming out of his hand. He knew how to make it look good too. He'd already had a broken arm, and it was the same arm. So he was crying, "It's my same arm, it's my same arm."

My daddy saw it, and he took me in there and whupped me, "Why you throw that rock? Why you throw that rock?" Whupped me!

THE FULLERTON FAMILY lived right across the street from us, originally from Mississippi. I grew up with Little Studie, their youngest son. The mother had family still living down in Mississippi. We heard from her about an incident that happened to her family in Mississippi.

A couple of her brothers had just got out of church, and they stopped in to get gas. They had some sort of credit deal with the station owner so they could pay the bill afterwards. After they got the gas, one of the brothers told the guy, "Put that on my daddy's bill."

But the guy in the station told them, "Your daddy don't have credit here no more." Like that. "You are gonna have to pay for the gas."

They said they didn't have any money.

The guy got smart with them and said, "Well then, I guess I'll have to take this battery." He raised the hood and was going to take the battery. One of the brothers got out and slammed the hood back down. The guy went back into the station, got a gun, came back out and shot in the car! They had a gun in the car, but the brother who had the gun was scared to shoot back. The other brother said, "What's wrong with you? This guy is going to kill us. You going to let this man kill us?" He grabbed the gun from his brother and shot and killed the guy.

They took off. They went back to the house, told some of the cousins what had happened, said they were getting out of town.

The cousins said, "Well, we ain't did nothing." They stayed.

The two brothers came to Bessemer, saw their sister, who lived across from us. We heard the brothers went out West when they left Bessemer, but the Fullertons never talked about that much.

It was the KKK that had started up something to cut their daddy's bill off. Their daddy had a little money that came down the generations. He was mixed. One of this family's relatives going back was the slave master's black son. He would have been born in slavery, that generation. Some times when it was like that, the slave master left their black kids some money. So the family had a little money passed down—plus some land, a nice big house. Maybe the KKK was mad about that.

Later, we heard that the KKK went and beat up their father and put him in jail after the two brothers left, like he had done something—locked him up and burnt his house down. Then they took one of the cousins and lynched him in a tree, just shot him, shot holes in one of the cousins because they couldn't find the two brothers.

I heard this family had already had a problem with the

KKK in the 1920s. The KKK had come by shooting at them, and they shot back. They killed somebody, too. The family had to hide out in the woods. The neighbor who lived next door to us—an older black woman, older than my grandmother—she told us this part of it.

Anyway, our neighbor across the street got the FBI into the case, with her father still in jail. I don't know what all happened, but they got the father out of jail. All those years I never heard any more about that. Maybe they didn't want to talk about it.

After I left Bessemer, when I went back to see my mother, I used to go down and see my friend's mother and father. Little Studie had moved away, but his mother and father moved right down the street from where they used to live, and when I'd go home, I'd go by and talk with them, and they'd be glad to see me. They went to the same church my family went to, Bethlehem Church. I guess they both probably have passed by now. I don't know, but a few years ago, they were still living at that place and I stopped by. Ninety-some years old. Pushing a hundred then. They were much older than my mother.

GROWING UP, there was always family—cousins, aunties, brothers. I don't even know how many cousins I had. But there was always someone around. My mother had eight sisters and five brothers. Except for one sister and one brother, they were all younger than her. Some weren't much older than me. My father had quite a few brothers and sisters also. And most of them had kids. My grandmother on my mother's side had almost a hundred grandkids, plus all the great-grandkids.

MY FAMILY had to bring my grandfather up to Bessemer. I was about ten or eleven. He had been poisoned down in Gainesville. They said this guy, Cable Sanders, who owned an old bull, was over there drinking, and they thought Cable put something in my granddaddy's drink. Cable and my granddaddy may have been into something, maybe about a woman, I don't really know. Whatever the poison was, people were talking, saying it had something to do with voodoo.

A lot of black people then were into that voodoo. They took him to a doctor in Bessemer, and the doctor said he didn't know what it was, said there was nothing he could do for my granddaddy.

So my mother and my grandmother brought him to this woman in Birmingham—she was from a family of the voodoos, the people who go all the way back to Africa. They knew about certain poisons and roots and plants they used way back in Africa. Down through the generations, the parents just passed it right on down to their kids. They were supposed to be the voodoo crowd.

This voodoo woman in Birmingham washed his face with something, and gave him something, told him to take that. When they brought him in to her, they said he was all bent over, couldn't straighten up. They had to lift him out of the car. My mother said it seemed like he got better that same day they took him over to the voodoo woman.

There may be some truth to it, that these voodoos know about different poisons and they know what to give you to deal with them. Doctors know a lot about these things now, but the doctors black folks had back then didn't know much.

Those roots and plants the voodoos were using—they said this understanding came from Africa. Only the ones in a certain tribe—the witch doctors, whatever they called them—knew about these things, coming down through their family.

This voodoo stuff came especially from Louisiana. The family used to call it hoodoo, not voodoo, but it's all about the same. Some people still talk about believing in it, certain things about it. People didn't understand all the means of it, so they pushed it further than what it really could do, but those roots and plants had some relationship to sicknesses. When the slaves came from Africa, they brought that knowledge with them, and they brought some of those plants.

Five
Down to the Farm in Gainesville

EVERY SUMMER SINCE I WAS about three or four years old, up to when I was twelve, my brothers and me would go down to the farm in Gainesville and stay the whole three months. Then, one day, someone would come down and get us. That was when school started back.

A lot of times, my daddy would take us down to Gainesville. Or Ma'Dear would be going down there, and we would go with her on the train. The train didn't have a route to go through Gainesville, so we would go right on through to Epps, which was right at the bottom of Alabama, going into Mississippi. She would find somebody and they would take us back to Gainesville.

She knew a lot of the people down there. If they were going to Gainesville, they would take us, drop us off. Those little towns are close together. At that time, you didn't have to know the people. If they were going to Gainesville, you got a ride. One of those things. We gave them a few dollars, and they took us to Gainesville or on out to the farm. Wasn't a problem.

Sometimes, my daddy would be coming down, and he

would pick us up and bring us back. If he didn't make the one trip down, he would make the other trip to bring us back.

That farm was about a hundred and some miles south, southwest of Bessemer. Tuscaloosa, Eutaw, then down to Gainesville, then about ten miles to the farm. Just farmland and little towns—that's all it was at that time. Gainesville had about four or five stores, like one of those old cowboy movies. Really, it didn't have as many stores as one of the old Westerns. A little police station, a little post office. That's about it. Kids used to go there on the week-ends, go to the store, get a soft drink, hang out there. It was just a little town.

IN THE DEPRESSION, people in Gainesville had lost all that they had put in the banks. After that, they wouldn't put their money in banks. They would stash it and hide it in the back of the house, under the house, bury it behind trees. This is what my great-grandfather did, he hid his money in the house. He lived in a big house that used to be the master's house, the plantation owner's house. He had some money stashed, and the house caught fire. Other people there, my granddaddy and other relatives, wouldn't let him go back in there. They knew if he got in there he would never be able to get out, and they weren't fixing to go in because the place was really burning. So he couldn't get his money. It burned up. I think they built another house on that same spot. I didn't see the house burn down, but I heard stories about it and I used to see some of that wood that was all burnt from the fire. The house they built was where I used to go stay with my grandfather.

I remember my great-grandfather walking around on his walking cane. I really don't know much about him, but I remember him. I can remember seeing him a few times when I was down there, but it wasn't too long after that he passed. He died when I was small, so I didn't know him that well.

THEY CALLED MY GRANDFATHER Hardware. His name was William Ware. But they called him Hardware. He was like in the song—wherever you lay your hat is your home. He was all over the place, over here and over there with different women. I think that's why he got that name. He was my mother's father, but he had a daughter by my daddy's mother. Hardware was the father of one my daddy's sisters. So that's my mother's half sister, but they always just said sisters. Plus, he was a man who didn't take very much off of other people. So this all had to do with his name.

One time, the sheriff picked him up and put him in jail, saying he had a gun. But his brother came and got him out. His brother worked for one of the big landowners that held most of the land around there, almost like the old plantation owner. Coming down through the generations from slavery, that same white family still owned the land. Since my grandfather's brother worked for one of the top big owners in the area, he could do just about anything he wanted and mostly get away with it. That's why he knew he could go to this little-town sheriff and tell him, "Let my brother go. You got the wrong one. He don't even carry no gun. I'm the one that carries the gun."

The sheriff knew who he worked for. My grandfather's brother was just letting the sheriff know that the big landowner LET him carry a gun. Wouldn't be no problem with him carrying a gun. The sheriff didn't want any problem with the guy who owned all the land. That guy owned the police station, too, everything. The sheriff wouldn't have a job if he messed with his boy, locked him up. So he let my grandfather out, just like that.

My grandfather was still a young man when that happened. I don't think I was alive yet when that happened. But my mother and my father and some of my aunties talked about it.

37

MY GRANDFATHER and his brother used to share the land. His brother may have had a little bit more than my grandfather did. Then they had the pasture gaps where they kept the livestock, one on the west side of their farms and one on the east side, where they had some horses and mostly cows. They used them together.

My granddaddy and his brother worked the land, sharecropping it for the master's kids, who still owned the land after the master died. I don't know exactly how it worked, but a lot of time my grandmother and grandfather were getting ripped off. During the year, they'd go into Gainesville and Epps and get different stuff they needed. The landowner would pay for it and put it on his bill. Once their farming was over for the year, and they sold cotton and maybe some corn, they would pay up the debt they owed. And they paid the landowner his share. The landowner would rip them off. When the time came to pay up at the end of the season, they sold their crop and got nothing back. By the time they gave that money to the landowner, they had nothing at the end of the year. That went on year after year. That's what the sharecropping was: they ain't got nothing left.

After my grandfather left, his brother took over all the land. And they said he finally bought some land.

I went down there once when I was a teenager, and a friend of ours went down to Gainesville with us. When we got there, he says, "Whose land you say that was?"

I told him, "My uncle, man."

"Where's your uncle?"

"He's in the field."

"What?"

He was a talker, this friend was. He figured if all this land belonged to my uncle, then he wouldn't be out there in the field. But my grandfather's brother was out there picking cotton. It was cotton season. They were all out there, his wife and kids, younger kids, out there picking cotton.

EVERY SUMMER, my mother left us there with her mother and younger sisters and brothers who were still living down there on the farm. Later on, all of them moved to Bessemer. But five of my aunties were still down there when we were kids. They used to help take care of us kids for my mother— her younger sisters, Lou, Ann, Bea, Clara Mae, Delores. Finally, there was nobody there but the last sisters, Delores and Lou, and a couple of my mother's brothers. Then one of the brothers, Elbert, moved to Tuscaloosa.

My mother's youngest brother, Jamie Ware, was only six years older than me. He was the baby boy, out of fourteen, a year and something older than Delores, the baby girl. When we went down to Gainesville, we would hang out with him. Jamie would go with his older brother, Elbert, and some other older kids. And because we were all with Jamie, we could go. So that means now the older brother's got Jamie and all these little kids going with them.

He'd tell Jamie, "Well you take those kids back."

Jamie didn't want to go back, so Elbert jumped on him, stomped his feet, hurt his toes. One of his toes was bleeding. I think Elbert may have had his shoes on.

After Elbert did that, jumped on my uncle Jamie's toes, Elbert and his friends took off, left us. They were just going swimming I think, but they just didn't want to be bothered with us. Younger kids, you know.

WE LIKED TO GO down there every summer. We did the farm stuff, you know how they do, hoe and chop in the fields, cut grass, pick cotton, see after the livestock. My grandparents had cows, horses, mules, so we fed them and carried slops out to the pigs and hogs. I used to go with my grandmother and feed them. I learned how to churn milk, how to churn and lift butter off the top. I remember going to the pasture with my aunties to milk the cows early in the morning. Sometimes my youngest aunties would churn the milk and show us how the cream starts to turn, come up looking like butter. Not there yet, but it's close. They lifted it so they would know when they could stop, when it be done.

That's how they got the butter. You churn, churn, churn, and all that butter will come up and just lay right on top of the milk. You scoop it off and put it in a dish. So we did that.

And we went fishing. When the farming stuff was over, crops over with, we went fishing just about every day. At least five days a week.

At night, we would fry the fishes whole, just chop their heads off and fry them in lard in a pan in the fireplace. It was nice. We would sit there eating those little fishes, talking and telling stories.

We'd be telling them about Bessemer, what was going on. We'd be schooling my cousins, telling them about what's happening in the city. They didn't know.

That's what made it so interesting, especially to my grandmother. The aunties all called her Mun. So we called her Mun. She'd be really into it, sitting forward, trying to catch everything we were saying, don't miss nothing.

While we were eating the fishes, Mun would say, "Now y'all gonna have to stop going fishing every day. You boys gonna use up all my lard." Like we caught too many fish— and she was sitting there eating the fish right along with us. That was fun.

One night we were talking, sitting around, Mun was telling us this story about riding a horse or a mule, probably a mule. Women were supposed to ride sidesaddle back then, wearing dresses the way they did. But it was raining, and she had to get on, get in the house before the storm kicked in. She sure enough was going to throw her leg over that mule and ride like a man, keep her head down on that mule like the guys running a race.

Lang Ware, (Mun) Sam's grandmother later in her life.

WHEN WE WEREN'T going fishing, we visited our cousins on my daddy's side. We used to go over there and hang with them. One cousin, Raymond, was three years and some older than me. His younger brother was only about a year and something older than me. I could get next to him wrestling. But I couldn't do nothing with Raymond, the older brother—he was real strong. He would throw me.

Just as quick as he threw me, I would get right back up and say, "Want to try it again? Let's do it again."

His daddy came out there and saw us and thought it may be a problem. If one of us got hurt, there was no doctor there. And they didn't have a car. So if we got hurt, they had to go ten miles to get us to a doctor, in a wagon, pulled by two mules. That's what they were using, a wagon with mules, because they didn't have a car. Raymond's daddy said, "You better stop throwing that boy, I can't take him to no doctor if you hurt him or break his arm." I must have been about ten or eleven.

WE LEARNED HOW to use certain words, sounds really. My granddaddy would make a certain sound, "whee, whee," and his dogs would come. My Uncle Charlie would go "whoo, whoo," a sound like that, and his dogs would start to come running.

A farmer nearby by the name of Cable had a bull. That bull came over in the pasture where we were. He just jumped the fence and was in there, running at us. So we got into the fenced-off spot where they milk the cows. In that area, the fence was built up higher, so he couldn't jump that fence. But he just ran around it. So we called the dogs, "whoo, whoo," and those dogs came running and got on that bull. They were on his legs. One grabbed on his face, bit him, tore something off his face. He was bleeding. Those dogs were hanging onto him. Then they ran him. He jumped back over the fence, but even then, when he jumped the fence, they went on chasing him. He was going back toward home, and they still ran him on past Uncle Charlie's house, past the pasture gap. They ran him home.

Then again, we were going to visit a cousin, I forget his name now. He was kin to Grace—she married my brother Ocie later on. He used to cook us food when we'd come down. So we were going to visit him. We had to go past that area with that same bull. That sucker saw us and, man, there he comes. He came to the fence and stopped and started running along the fence. We were running along one side and he was running on the other side. Then all of a sudden, he would jump the fence and come over on the other side where we were. But when he did that, it wasn't no problem. When he would jump over on this side, we hit the ground and we rolled under the fence to the other side. So then we were running down on the other side.

We were smart enough not to run away from the fence because then he could get us. We would move away from the fence a little bit, and then he would jump back over. We were trying to see what he would do because we would have to come away from the fence pretty soon to cross the road to get over to our cousin's house. That's where that sucker would be ready to get us. The fence was headed in my cousin's direction but we still would have to go away from it at some point to get there. We made him jump a couple of times, and I guess he got tired of it. We finally got down there to the gap right before the road where my cousin lived. Then the bull stopped and was just looking at us. So we took off and ran to our cousin's house. A bad old bull.

THE LAST TIME I went down and stayed, I was twelve years old. That year I stayed with my Uncle Charlie Ware. My grandparents, just the year before, had moved to Bessemer. They left the farm and they were staying with one of my aunties. My Uncle Charlie had moved from the farm to

Bessemer, then he went to Detroit, worked there for a while at Ford I think, but then he came back down to Gainesville and opened up a little café in his house and was selling liquor. Moonshine. He had a restaurant selling food and liquor and had dice games. When the cops started coming by, Charlie figured it was too much of a risk, so they had to shoot dice in the woods—shot their dice there with lanterns, kept it dark, shooting in the dark.

Most people wouldn't mess with Charlie. He wasn't taking nothing off of nobody. He was one of those guys who would fight.

The last year I was in Gainesville, I noticed a guy who lived right across from Charlie, talking against him. My uncle was thinking this guy was cool, but behind my uncle's back, he was talking to some other guy about him.

I was there, but they must have thought I wasn't going to get it because I was a young boy. But I got it right away, what this guy said. They were thinking I was a farm boy. But I was from the city. I knew more than they did.

We taught them when we went down there. When you are on the farm, you are very confined. You don't know about all that's going on in the city. But I knew about New York, Chicago, Cleveland, Akron. We had relatives going to these places, coming back and telling us. I knew all about these places. I hadn't been there, but I knew because the family was going to places like that. And folks were doing some of the same things in Bessemer that they were doing in the big city. But they weren't doing it down there on the farm. Nowhere to do it. That's why we were way ahead of them.

These guys thought they were talking to a little farm boy, so they could say what they wanted and Charlie wouldn't hear it. But Charlie did hear it, because no sooner did I hear it, I made sure I went right back and told my uncle what they said.

"Damn that ..." my uncle said. He was pissed.

I said, "Yeah, that's what they said. I guess they against you." I hipped Charlie to be more alert.

So Charlie was ready then. One time after that, we were in town, and he had some words with one of them. Because he knew about them now, he went right home. He didn't know what they might have, so he got his shotgun and his pistol. He came back, but nothing happened. But he was ready.

When I was going around with Charlie, one of the women he was going to see asked him, "Whose boy is that, Charlie?"

"That's my son."

"Charlie, stop lying. That must be one of your sisters' boys."

CHARLIE WAS something else. He bought a new 1950 Chevrolet, paid cash for it. He was working two or three days a week with the loggers, cutting logs—that's all he worked. He told me his boss asked him, "Charlie, how in the hell you bought that car and paid cash?"

"Well, I saved it up," said Charlie.

If he was saving money it wouldn't have been a new car—since he wasn't working a full week. It messed with the boss that Charlie paid cash for that car.

When I was down there, I went to one of his stills with him, where he was making that liquor. Some guy he was working with taught him how to make it. They had these big old fifty-gallon drums and small barrels right nearby. They built a fire under that big drum, then they put corn, sugar, water and I don't know what else in the drum. That's what they were making the liquor out of, corn. When they heated it up, and it got a certain temperature, be hot and steaming, it started running out of that drum, out of a little pipe, into a barrel. I tasted it when it first started coming out of the drum, it wasn't much strong at all, just tasted like a little wine.

But they let it sit in the barrels some days, and it went to a hundred and some proof.

He used to make it out in the woods, not far from where he was living. The cops came through there once. Charlie and the others had just left, and I think the cops found the still but Uncle Charlie was gone. He had to relocate then. Once the cops find it, can't go back there no more.

CHARLIE'S WIFE worked right down the road from their place. She worked for some white land owner, and she got milk and butter and other things to take home.

One time, a couple years earlier, we went over there with the youngest uncle, Jamie, to get milk and other stuff. Four of us were in the car, Jamie, me, Ocie and my cousin Carlos. Uncle Jamie was a teenager then, but we weren't. He was driving his brother Charlie's car.

A little boy came out, about six maybe, a little white boy. He came out there, walking around, looking in the car. He came around to the driver's side where my uncle was. He looked in the car, then he asked my uncle, "How many niggers in that car?"

My uncle said, "Four."

The boy walked away and I said, "Why you tell that boy that?"

"Well, that's what they call us."

Here we were, about nine or ten, and he was fifteen or sixteen, driving Charlie's car. But he was so slow. That was all he had to say, "Well that's what they call us."

Six
The Italians

THE ITALIANS WERE DIFFERENT than the whites. We grew up with them, Dee and the other Italian guys—I forget some of the names now, but we all ran together, up there on 19th and 18th Streets, between 10th and 11th Avenues. We knew all these Italian kids. We played together, played in the street, ball and other stuff with all these guys. Laughing with them. Going by the sawmill. They could go to the white schools and we couldn't, but when they came out of school, they were playing with us, because their stores were right there where we were.

They lived right next door to the store, most of the Italians did, until sometime they may move out and rent it out to some blacks in the neighborhood. Most of them had to live next door to their stores. All the young Italian boys, we grew up with them.

I know one guy, this Italian dude, he was much bigger than me. When we go head-up wrestling, he couldn't handle me. Because he didn't know what I knew. I'd have him on the ground. Whoop! But when it came to football, I couldn't stop him. When he got the ball, come through there running, he would knock me down and be gone. I forgot what his name was, too. He used to come down there all the time, and we used to play down there on the west side of the bridge. We all used to go up on top of the sawmill buildings, black and Italian.

We used to play with other Italian kids, up on the next block, on 9th Avenue and 18th Street. I forget some of the names now—DC and all of them. There were Italian kids up on 19th Street, out on the corner of 9th Alley—their family had a store there. Then there was another family, they had a store right on 19th Street and 10th Avenue. Some of those stores were less than a block apart—one around that way, then another one right on this corner. All those little markets. You go on down to 11th Avenue and 19th Street, there's another store. Then you go on down to 12th Avenue, on the corner of 19th Street, there's another store. Then on to 18th Street, and 12th Avenue, too, there's a store on that corner. Just about every other block. And the Italian families ran all those stores.

All around Bessemer, the Italians ran the stores. Just little markets, neighborhood grocery stores. The Italian kids didn't hardly play with the white kids, just a few blocks away, they played with the black kids. There was prejudice against them too. I guess the Italians understood that they were being discriminated against, too, just like the blacks were. I can see in the actions of the kids, they were so much different.

MY BROTHERS WILLIE AND JESSE and a cousin, James Ware, used to work at one of these stores near us, helping clean up, not regular, just temporary when the store needed help. They were maybe eleven and nine. One day, one of them came across money hidden in a coat pocket. The owner's son Sammy had stashed the money—he was stealing money from his dad. His plan was to get him a car. Maybe he could have got the car later on, but by stealing extra money from his dad, he could get the car faster. He was stashing the money in an old coat in one of the back rooms.

Willie and James happened to find the coat. They saw this money, so they each took a few dollars, ten dollars or so.

Willie told Jesse, and Jesse went in and got it all. They had to talk him out of it, "Don't take all his money!" Finally, he went and put most of it back.

Sammy came up and found some of his money gone, and they say he was crying. He knew they had got it because they were the only ones back there. But he didn't press the issue because he had stolen it from his dad. So he let it go.

I went in and helped out some times, putting things away, taking garbage out, even when I was five or six—especially when Sammy and his sister Rosalie weren't there, and it was just the old man. He used to pay us in fruit or candy.

The old man had a broken window, where he had apples and oranges and other fruit. All he had was a cardboard where the hole was, instead of replacing the glass. Sometimes we would come up there and push that little cardboard through that hole and get us an apple or an orange. Small as our hands were, we could just reach up through that hole and get us an orange or an apple and then get back and go up the alley. He never saw us.

The store was on 18th Street and 9th Alley. We were on 10th Avenue near 18th Street. So we could come right out the back of the house into 9th Alley, come down just half a block, and the store was right there. The daughter Rosalie would come back around and play with us in the back yard before she got married. She knew my mother that well. She was much older, but she still would come around there playing with us, the kids.

Sammy, her brother, played with the older black kids, but she would come around and play with us. Later on she married Joe Gardenia. I think he was working in Birmingham, some kind of sales person. He married her, then they took over the store. Sammy moved out and went somewhere. The old man just turned the store over to his daughter and her husband, and they took it over. That's when I got to know Joe Gardenia, after he married Rosalie.

JOE GARDENIA WAS A LITTLE BIT crazy. He made a little old thing out of wire—it was almost like a slingshot shape. He tied some rubber on one end, put a washer in the middle of it, then tied it on the other end, hanging loose. He would turn that washer around and around until it was tightened. He would put it up under his butt, sit on it, then raise up and it'd go RRUMMMPP! Sounds like a fart. Just like that. He thought it really was funny. He finally showed us what it was.

So we made those things. My daddy was in the room once, talking to one of his cousins, and we were sitting on the floor, down by them. I made that washer go RRUMMMPP—made that farting sound.

Daddy's cousin looked, but he didn't say nothing.

Then I went RRUMMMPP again.

Daddy's cousin couldn't help himself: "What? What? What's all that noise? Why you let that boy sit there and do that?"

Daddy just backed up. He had that smile on his face, he knew what was going on.

We were rolling. That's what we got from Joe Gardenia. I could make one of those little things right now. When you sit on it, on the floor, nothing happens because that washer can't turn when you are on it. But when you ease up off of it, that washer can turn, RRUMMMPP! And if you were on something that makes it sound loud, it was so funny.

BEFORE I GOT TO BE a teenager, I was working for a little place that just sold the ice cream. One day I was there working with one of my cousins John Dew. He was talking about some shoes he saw, telling us where it was, "It's that dago's down there."

One of the Italian guys who owned the ice cream place said to my cousin, "Hey, come here, let me talk to you. Are you a nigger?"

"No."

"Well you know that guy down there at the shoe store? He's not no dago either. He's Italian. He's no dago. Just like you ain't no nigger. They say that to put us down, just like they put you down."

We didn't know the difference, we all would say that. My cousin said it right in front of some of the Italians. He didn't know. When you're a kid you don't know. We thought that's what they were, dagos. But that Italian guy called him on it. And we finally got it.

Seven
About the Dew Drop Inn

SOME WHITE GUYS had been throwing rocks at my friends, sitting on the bridge. Our friends ran down to the Dew Drop Inn, knowing they had all kinds of back-up at the Dew Drop Inn.

It was a little café, owned by Otis Brown. He had a grandson used to be there too, working there in the daytime at a young age. They called him Bill. During the day, Bill would let us come down there and hang out, play pool. We played the music box, cut up and danced a little bit. But at night times, we weren't supposed to be in there. When we got to be teenagers, we tried to hang out there at night too, but Otis Brown would put us out. My uncles and my aunties and some of my older cousins would all be hanging down there. Otis Brown knew the family. He used to be a tough guy, but he didn't want to be messing with the family. He had said, "Too many of them. Even though they are a lot of fools, there are too many of them."

So there came the white guys in a car and a truck, followed my friends down there. But that was a mistake because all of us were standing out in front when they got down there. These fools were going to drive right up on us. So we started throwing bricks and shit at them. Man, they took off flying.

I grew up seeing this shit, seeing all the stuff that came from this prejudice and racism. One of my uncles, Henry

52

Ware, was drunk over at the Dew Drop Inn, and the cops came along and made him crawl on the ground. I didn't see that, but some of my aunties saw it, and they talked about it. He used to get so mad, he cut the trees with his knife. But he crawled. Uncle was afraid of the cops.

SINCE I WAS A LITTLE KID, I grew up watching people fight each other. People were going through a lot of troubles anyway, then someone right there with them gets them upset, says the wrong thing, does the wrong thing. It gets them going.

Somebody says something.

Somebody else says, "Don't say that no more."

Sometimes neither one is going to walk away.

A fight can turn out bad and nasty. If they just tussle and hit each other, it's not much. But sometimes people come up another way, and someone gets hurt or even killed. A lot of times, other people step in, especially if they know the people.

Bea, one of my mother's sisters, got into a fight with one of my cousins at the Dew Drop Inn. This was when I was already about fourteen or fifteen. It was all in this big family. This one cousin, Punkie we called her, was on my daddy's side—my daddy's sister's daughter. Bea's husband Joe was messing around with Punkie. And my auntie found that out. Punkie and my auntie were down at the Dew Drop Inn and got in a fight down there. They both had knives. I think my cousin never did get a chance to cut my auntie, but my auntie cut her about three times. My cousin was bleeding like crazy, she was cut in the face.

Some of the family grabbed my auntie, and some grabbed my cousin, and they took one this way and one that way. "Now y'all stop this."

Bea was a little woman too. She was about the smallest of the sisters, but she was tough. She was worse than my mother when it came to fighting.

Not long before that, this other incident happened. I was playing cards just down the street from where I lived. Bea got into it with her old man. Bea had sneaked around through the alley to catch up with him, to catch him with Punkie.

The neighbor woman—we were playing cards there at her house for pennies, nickels and dimes—she happened to look out the back and she said, "Come here, ain't that your auntie?"

"Yeah, looks like it."

"You better get on out there, he's got that big old stick hitting at her."

He had a big brush-like stick, like a tree limb. He hit Bea a couple times with it already. And she had a knife.

So I ran out the back and went down there. Bea was just crying and had a knife in her hand, steady trying to get up on him. Joe with this long stick, Bea with a knife, crying.

So I said "Come on, Auntie Bea, come on."

She finally stopped, and Joe still had his stick saying, "You better take her home, you better take her home."

So we walked off to the house. Oh boy.

Eight
A Black Teenager in the Jim Crow South

EVEN BEFORE I WAS A TEENAGER, I was working for a little ice cream business. The owners were two Italian brothers. They bought and sold ice cream, popsicles, ice cream sandwiches, things like that. We rode on a bike with these little carts, just one wheel up front and two behind, peddling it around in the neighborhood. Before they let you work there, one of the brothers would check to see if you could count and give the right change back.

One time, I was selling ice cream in the community in the white area.

A little white boy came to get some ice cream. When he got his ice cream, he said to me, "Mister Nigger, are you coming back tomorrow?"

I understood there wasn't no hate in him. This kid didn't hate black people. He was smiling and happy to see me, and that's why he said "Mister Nigger." So I didn't mess with him.

But somebody was already teaching him to become a racist. He just didn't know it yet.

MY BROTHER WILLIE and two of my cousins used to sell ice cream on the street for that same company. James Ware, one of the cousins, got into a fight with the youngest son of one of the owners. The youngest son was messing

55

with my cousin so they got to fighting. My cousin threw him down and beat him, not serious, but got him down and socked him in the face.

The guy who owned the place told his son, "I told you to leave James alone."

My cousin came back home proud, talking about it, how he beat that white boy.

His daddy, Levi Ware, said, "What? What? You had a fight with that white boy? Don't you know those people could come in here and kill us all?" That's what his daddy said to him. And his daddy whipped him.

My cousin felt so proud that he had whipped the white boy. But his own daddy turned around, because he was afraid, and whipped his own son for fighting the white boy. Levi was married to my daddy's younger sister.

WHEN I REACHED teenage, it seemed like the whites had much more rights than we did. We had to ride at the back of the buses and street cars and trains. We couldn't swim in the same pools with whites. We couldn't eat in the same restaurants. We couldn't sit and watch the same movie in theaters.

I WAS IN THE NINTH GRADE, in high school, and they were talking about integrating the schools. This was in the mid-1950s.

The history teacher told us that WE weren't ready for integration. I'll never forget this. He told us if they integrated the schools right then, and we went into the big school, the whites' school, we would start two years or more behind the whites because the books they gave us put us two years behind the whites. If we would go into integrated schools, we would be way back, two grades behind.

He was saying we weren't ready—not that integration wasn't a good thing, just that we weren't ready. "They've got you two books behind the white kids. That means, if you're integrated, you are going to be two grades behind."

THE NEXT YEAR, I QUIT SCHOOL when I turned sixteen. I went to work at the Superior Ice Cream Company. We had just moved down to Jonesboro. Superior Ice Cream was the first real job I had. I liked to work at Superior. It was owned by an Italian family too. I did everything at the ice cream company—worked there making popsicles and the ice cream cones that you put nuts on, and that ice cream on a stick, chocolate covered, different popsicles, strawberry or whatever, ice cream sandwiches. Lot of times, I moved around. We put trays on this line, where it froze up. By the time they got to the end, they were frozen. The guy who worked on the other end pulled them out. He shot them down to the next person, who took them and dumped them into something like a tray. Then some women were working right there, putting them in a bag. Then there was someone taking the bags and putting them into the cold storage. So I worked on both ends. About twenty some people worked there, with the bosses and other jobs. And there were a couple truck drivers.

I WAS HANGING OUT at my sister-in-law's restaurant— we started to call it "The Square." I was sixteen. Someone came by The Square and said there was a bad accident on 19th Street, so we went up there to see what was happening.

There was a crowd, whites and blacks, and a lot of cops were all over the place. The minute we got there, a black guy and a white guy were about to get it on because of a woman's wig in the street.

The white guy yelled, "It must be Autherine Lucy's hair." Autherine Lucy was the first black woman to attend the University of Alabama at Tuscaloosa.

The black guy said right back to him, "It must be some of

57

your mammy's hair!" Right away a cop said, "Alright, now let's stop this."

There were rumors out about riots, and the cops were scared. I came out with a pocketful of bullets and my father's little old piece in my pocket. I wasn't the only one.

ONE DAY, MY BOSS at Superior was talking about Nat King Cole and the KKK. Nat King Cole was supposed to be performing in Birmingham in 1956. The KKK had planned to lynch him when he came there. The police had quite a few undercover officers in that building. The KKK didn't know that. About eight of the KKK came in to get him. There were supposed to be about a hundred of them ready to lynch him after the eight snatched him and took him somewhere. That was the plan. But when three of the KKK came up on the stage to grab him, the undercover cops ran up on the stage too and grabbed the KKK. Even a white woman there was swinging her purse and saying "You're not gonna hurt Nat!" Swinging her purse on those guys.

After this fight, they arrested some of the KKK. The police went in the trunk of the KKK's car. They said these suckers had weapons, all kind of guns in the trunk of the car. They found other cars that belonged to somebody else, with weapons and ropes they used for lynching.

My boss said, "I can't understand that shit, now if you don't want to see nobody, why go? Why would three thousand people come out to see him if they didn't want him here?"

But the KKK didn't want any black man coming to Alabama and perform. Nat King Cole was just that popular, very popular back in '56. Even that white woman was up there swinging her purse, "No, you're not gonna take Nat." My boss was Italian.

MY COUSIN RAYMOND came up to Bessemer from the farm and was working at the ice cream company. He was about nineteen, three years older than me. When we were wrestling, I was almost about up with him. He was still getting me but I could get up with him. And he knew it. When I got seventeen, he couldn't get me down any more. We were up at the job, in the bathroom tussling. We didn't have that much area and time, and we had to go back to work. We were just tussling around. I didn't get him but he couldn't get me either. So we just cut it. That's when he told me he had noticed the difference. He knew that I had really changed and was faster than him and just as strong. He told me later on that he knew I had gone past the day when he could deal with me.

I WAS ALWAYS RUNNING INTO IT with the cops. They would see us, pull us over. "Teenager," they had in their mind—that thing about teenagers. We would be driving my daddy's Cadillac, and they really didn't like that. When I was a teenager, Daddy used to let me have it sometimes, drive around to The Square or over to my girl's house. They'd stop me, "Whose car is this, boy?" They knew whose car it was, but they'd stop me anyway. Just messing with me.

Once, when I was seventeen, I had the car and was over at my girlfriend's house. The police just sat there and sat there. I waited two hours or more. I knew when I came out, they were going to pull me over. They were sitting in the alley with the front end of their car just sticking out. I knew it was them. They were waiting for me to come out because I was driving that Cadillac. So I said I was going to sit there until they leave, but they wouldn't ever leave. So finally, I had to go. Time I got in the car, here they come. They were waiting on that Cadillac to move. Trailed me all the way home.

When I got to the house, they asked me, "Whose car is that?"

"It's my daddy's car."

"What you doing, bringing your daddy a drink or something?"

"He don't drink."

"Well what you got in that trunk?"

"Ain't nothing in that trunk."

"Well open it up."

I opened the trunk up. He looked all through the trunk. There wasn't anything in it. So he said something like, "Well, OK then, you have a good night. Bye." Like he was polite or something.

They sat there all of two hours, maybe longer, killing time, just to be messing with me.

A COUSIN OF MINE from the farm, Roy, used to come up to Bessemer a couple times a year and stay with us. One night we were out—Roy, a friend Olds and me—and a gang of guys jumped us. Some guy hit Roy in the mouth, busted his lip.

He was pissed off about that, so he bought him a pistol, a .25. He had it on him when we went down to The Square.

We pulled the car right up in front of my girl's house, going to park just a few houses down from the Square. Time we got out of the car, a cop drove up, "Hold it right there, boy."

I went on up to the porch of my girl's house, we hadn't done anything. But Roy was a little slow in this situation. He could have taken a couple more steps and threw it under the house. That was all he had to do, take a few more steps. It was dark. The cop wouldn't have seen him do it.

But Roy was a country boy. He stopped and walked back to the cop. Just got the gun last week, and this week got busted with it. The cop took the gun, took him to jail—cost him a couple hundred dollars to get out of jail.

The whites had guns too. They'd ride around in their

truck with their rifles and shotguns right behind their head, showing them around town. And most of them carried pistols. Everyone knew it. But the cops didn't come on to the whites the same way.

ANOTHER NIGHT, two guys, friends of mine, were walking on their way over to get a fish sandwich. I was at my girlfriend's house right nearby. These two door shakers came up—that's the name we gave them. When the police were walking around on the street, walking their beat, shaking doors and stuff like that, we called them door shakers. My brother Jesse gave them that name first.

Time my two friends got up to the corner, here come the door shakers, spotting lights on them, stopping them, asking them where they're going.

My friends tried to tell them they were going to get a fish sandwich. But the police patted them down. They didn't have anything on them, but the police went on harassing them, just because they wanted to.

I was thinking, "They're messing with my friends, let me mess with them. I'm going to give the police something to think about."

I was down in the dark, they didn't know who I was. I started to holler at the cops, "Hey, if you don't know me, you better get the hell off The Square 'cause I'm still wearing these elevens." (Kick your ass, you know.)

They asked my friends, "Who is that down there?"

One of them said, "Well I don't know, it's some guy. He may be drunk."

My brother Jesse used to mess with the cops. That's where I got that from. He was messing with them before he left to go in the Navy. So I took his place when he left. Mess with me, mess with y'all—he taught me that.

So I kept on talking. "I'm talking about you. With that little piece on your side. Blue uniform, with that little piece on your side, I'm talking to you."

One of them started to walk down where I was, so I got behind a big old tree in the yard, but I couldn't see them.

My girl friend's brother was there whispering to me, "He still coming."

So I walked down between the houses. They were what people called shotgun houses, you could walk right down between them. When I walked down between them to the back of the house, that cop came to the front, but no further. He wasn't coming down between those houses in the dark. He went back out to where his partner was.

The cops let my friends go because I was messing with them, they didn't know who it was, and they weren't going back there in the dark. When they left, I came back and sat on the porch.

WE HAD PROBLEMS with the cops all the time. Here's another one. We were racing down 20th Street—me and another friend. When we got down there about one block from my girl's house, I saw the door shakers come running out with their little flashlights. But my friend got up too close to them. When I saw them running with the spotlight, I stopped my car, hit reverse, Rrrrooom Rrrroooom, went flying backwards a block from 8th Avenue to 9th Alley. Shot up 9th Alley.

Then they shot. They told my friend, "You tell that boy, that friend of yours, the next time we gonna shoot IN that damn Cadillac." They did shoot, but they didn't hit the car. "Next time we gonna shoot in that damn Cadillac, he take off like that again."

They busted him for racing, speeding down the street. He got a ticket. But they didn't hit me. I got away. But they could have hit someone else in the street, shooting like that.

I THINK I WAS SEVENTEEN, the first time they took me to jail. I was with Ocie, my youngest brother. We had been to a teen-age club for a dance. That was 1956, and there was a curfew on at the time—for blacks. It wasn't for whites. We had to be off the street at nine o'clock unless we were nineteen or with an adult. It was about ten p.m. when we got out of the teen club. So we walked over to the café, The Square.

There were three sisters that ran this place. Their daddy leased it and turned it over to them. "Y'all need a job, here's your job. Run this." He worked at Pullman, the same place that my daddy worked at. Their daddy came by every once in a while and checked on it, but they ran it. The youngest was eighteen, the next was about twenty—my brother married this girl. And the oldest sister was about twenty-four. That was their job, they ran that place. They sold breakfast and dinners, and they had beer too at night. That was The Square for most young folks. Our spot. Young folk was running it, that's why we called it The Square.

Anyway we were sitting in there. It was about ten, I guess. But we weren't on the street. One of my cousins, who was old enough to be out, was there with us. He was going to drop us off. My older brother was home on a leave from the Navy, and I had on his pea coat, that long blue coat. And I had on dark pants and a hat. Not a sailor hat—but I had on his coat and I had on dark pants.

The police came in the café, asking how old we were. One asked my brother, "How old are you, boy?"

He told them nineteen. He was only fifteen.

"Show us your ID. Show us something with your name on it."

My brother pulled out his Social Security card and gave it to them.

"Boy, I need something with your age on it."

All these other young people sitting around were

watching us, and they just cracked up. Laughing. And the cops didn't like that shit. "I need something with your age on it, boy." People in the café were just rolling.

It was so shocking to them, how we talked to them and acted because most black people hadn't done that before. Folks didn't say nothing, they were scared, and they showed it. But we just came straight up, "What? What you talking about?" The white cops hadn't dealt with this before.

So alright, one asked me, "How old are you boy?" Then he asked, "Are you in the service?"

So I never did tell him how old I was—I was seventeen—I never gave him an age. I just told him I wasn't in the service. The first question, I didn't even relate to that one.

"So, you're not in the service, then whose coat you got on?" He saw the coat was new, and it was a Navy coat. He came back and said it again, "I asked you, whose coat that is."

A cousin of the girls running the place said, "Tell the man whose coat that is."

I said, "I done told this man already, it's my brother's coat."

The cops said, "You, you, come on, let's go."

They took Ocie and me out of the place. They were door shakers too, they weren't driving a patrol car yet. They were still street walkers. They took us out and hadn't got but a few feet away from the place, and they were juking me in the back with a billy club. "Walk up!"

When he did that, I started walking a little bit faster.

Then he did it again. "Boy I ain't gonna tell you to walk up again." He hit me in the back with that club.

I just reacted, turned around on him and said, "I don't know how fast you want me to walk."

Then they both pulled their guns. "You'll know when you're walking too fast, dammit, when you hear a bullet going over your head. Get on, nigger!" And they pushed me.

Then we walked from 20th Street up to 19th Street, but before we got to 19th Street, they started something up all over again, "You sure you're not in the service?"

"I told y'all I wasn't in no service."

"Well you sure talk like one of those smart ones just got back."

I hadn't ever been outside Alabama, but I "talk like one of those smart ones that just got back!" I guess they thought that I'd been trained, like in the service. But I'd never been out of Alabama, just been trained in the streets. I got that from Jesse.

Then they both pulled their guns again, saying, "You act like you want to run. Go ahead, nigger, run."

Both of them had their guns on me again. Fucking with me.

Ocie got nervous, telling me, "Don't run, don't run, they gonna shoot you."

Just about then, here come four young kids, younger than we were, white kids. When the cops saw them, at first they didn't know they were white. One of the cops said, "Here come four more." He started across the street, but no sooner than he got across the street, he realized they were white, and he turned around and came right on back.

Those white kids went right on walking, walked right on by. It was curfew, but it didn't mean nothing for them because they weren't black. We saw that right there.

The door shakers didn't have a car so they called for a car to pick us up. The car came down and took us to jail.

We were going up the stairs, and one of them came running. He hit me up side my head, knocked my hat off, Boom! "Nigger, you don't come in this jail with no hat on, nigger."

He could've just told me to pull the hat off, but he had to do something, get in something last, so he hit me. They threw us in jail and locked us up.

Ocie had a knife, a short one, and he went all the way into jail with that knife. I told him, "Man, get rid of it, they may search you again." So he put it under the mattress in the jail.

The next morning I called my work place. I was working then at the ice cream place. And I called home. I was supposed to be at work the next day. My boss sent a guy over to get me out of jail. That was pretty cool, wasn't it? My boss was Italian. When I left out of there I just went on to work. My mother came and got my brother out of jail. We both had to pay thirty dollars to get out of jail.

My mother took them to court on that one. She won the case. She got all the thirty dollars back for Ocie, and fifteen back out of the thirty that I paid. They weren't supposed to arrest us because we weren't on the street.

The judge asked the cops what happened, and they said, "Well, they were in this café."

"What were they doing? Were they drinking beer?"

"No, they weren't drinking beer, but beer was being drunk."

I think that's why I wound up paying fifteen dollars because I was in a place serving beer.

One of the cops told the judge, "Well, we asked them certain questions and all the others in the place, they was just laughing. And making a monkey out of us."

"What do you mean?"

"Well they was all laughing when we asked certain questions."

Then the lawyer my mother got showed that my brother shouldn't have been locked up, he was only fifteen.

The judge told the cops, "You're not supposed to lock them up when they are fifteen. You can take them to juvenile, but not to regular jail." Anyway we did get out of jail.

I WENT TO JAIL AGAIN, maybe that same year. I was out with this guy named Mayfield who worked at the ice cream place. I had just bought that Ford. We had been down to the Girl Scout camp where families went for picnics, drinking beer and wine. Coming back, I was speeding. I had a stick shift and two exhaust pipes on that Ford, and when I was coming down the hill I was flying. When I got up off it, the exhaust pipes went Pop, Pop, Pop, Pop, Pop! At the bottom, the cops were parked there, giving out tickets. They saw me coming down there, my brakes a little low. When I got down there I shifted down. I was trying to make the car stop. It revved up some and the brakes made that screeching noise, Rrrr, Rrrr.

"Something wrong with your brakes? Get out of the car." He went and got in the car, said, "Yeah these brakes is low. You was speeding. You was speeding down there, coming down that hill." He told me, "You, you go get in that car there." They had a patrol car parked there.

My friend Mayfield started talking. "Can't we go now?"

"No you can't go."

Mayfield came back and said something else.

"Is you drunk? You get in that car, too."

Mayfield came in that car cussing, "Those motherfuckers, man, fixing to take me to jail." They got me for speeding and the brakes, and they got him for under the influence. So they took me and Mayfield to jail. They didn't even handcuff us, they didn't think we were any problem. But they took us in anyway.

On our way to jail, Mayfield was still talking. He was sitting up in the front with the cop driving. I was in the back. Mayfield, sitting up there beside the cop, said, "Your buddy gave you a dirty deal."

The cop said, "What's that?"

"You know he didn't even much search me. I could have a gun or anything and just shoot you." That's what Mayfield said, just like that.

"What?"

Mayfield told him again.

The cop got nervous then. I could tell, I was in the back, looking at him—he got nervous. He was just going along with everything Mayfield said, until we got to the jail.

When he pulled into the jail parking lot, we got out of the car and went in the back of the building where they had a desk and security sitting there. That cop pushed Mayfield, "If you got a damn gun, you put it on the table right there."

Mayfield said, "I ain't got no gun."

They finally took us upstairs and locked us up. Okay, we were in there overnight again. For what? For nothing. For a traffic ticket.

I got out early morning, but they didn't like the way Mayfield was talking. So they kept him until the next day, said he was too high to get out.

I WENT TO JAIL with Mayfield another time. I was supposed to go to church that day, but I didn't go. I had to pick up my laundry and it wasn't ready. So I didn't get my clothes to wear to church. Mayfield called me. "Hey man, I want to go over to my girl's house." She lived in some little town southwest of Bessemer. "Man, could you take me over there?"

We went down there to these girls' house, and we sat around drinking for awhile. When we got set to leave, Mayfield wanted to drive the car, and I let him.

Coming through one of those little old towns, all these white Southern boys were out there, sitting down, squatting down—you know how those country boys do. Mayfield, coming through there, was going to show off. But he didn't know one of those boys was a sheriff, and that sheriff had a plain car sitting there. Mayfield didn't see that. He came down and made those loud pipes roar, and next thing we knew, here was this little car moving up on us. An old Ford. A real old car, older than my car, late 1940s, I think. Mayfield pulled over. "God damn."

So the sheriff told us to get out of the car. We got out. He told Mayfield, "Boy, you going to jail for speeding." Then he told me, "You look like you been drinking. You're going in for under the influence."

So I went to jail again. Mayfield called his friends, and they came to bail us out. But the cops said we had to stay there anyway, because we were still under the influence. We had to stay in there three hours before they let us out.

IN THAT TIME period, the young blacks weren't going along with the way things had been before. A lot of them weren't afraid of the cops. I had another cousin named Joseph, this one a little younger than me. The cops beat him up when he was eleven. But I didn't know about that until I read about it later on. I didn't even know he was a cousin until someone in the family told me. There was a picture of him in Jet magazine, how he looked with his face and head all wrapped up in bandages.

When he was seventeen, a cop was chasing him for some reason. He got his car into a dead end, couldn't get out. So they had him trapped. He got out of the car. The cop pulled his gun and was going to hit him with it. I guess Joseph just reacted, he wasn't going to let himself be hit in the head again. He grabbed the cop's gun and shot him. Joseph tried to get out of town, but he didn't make it. He was on the bus, but they caught up with him, took him off. He spent twenty-five or thirty years of his life in prison because he didn't want to be beat in the head again.

Nine
Starting to Leave Alabama

MY OLDEST BROTHER WILLIE took off for Detroit in 1953. My mother's brothers Jamie Ware and Charlie Ware were already there. And my mother's youngest sister, Delores, went up there too. My cousin Clarence Ware was up there. And so was another cousin on my daddy's side. Like most of the people leaving the South, they went so they could get a better job and get away from the racism. Willie was the first of my brothers to leave. He was eighteen.

Jesse left in 1955. He was already in some kind of unit like the National Guard. They gave him a uniform. But he wanted to go in the army. So he dropped out of that unit, then went and signed up for the Army. They called him to come in, but they were putting him in the Navy.

"Why you put me in the Navy, I didn't sign up for the Navy, I wanted the Army." He didn't want to be on a boat.

They told him he didn't have no choice. He was drafted. He was going to be on that boat. He was just stuck. Jesse was used to going around. Couldn't do that on the boat. And there weren't many blacks in the Navy.

Jesse was in there only a year and something. I guess he was a problem. They let him out. When you're a problem, they may let you out of there. In the Second War, they didn't put too many blacks into units that had guns. After Korea, they did. But when you're a problem, and you're black and got guns in your hands, they don't want you around.

A year or two later, Willie got drafted. He was in Detroit by that time. He didn't want to be in the military, from day one. He brought up all kinds of things, different diseases and problems he was having, one lie after another. They let him out of there too. He was in there for only a few months, a month or two right after basic training.

THE LAST OF 1957, I LEFT HOME. It was winter, and Superior Ice Cream cut back and laid me off. So I went to Detroit, stayed about six or seven months. I was eighteen.

I got to Detroit on New Year's Eve. They were shooting when I got there, the New Year had just come in. I came up from Bessemer on the bus and got a cab that took me to the wrong place. I had an address on East Euclid right off Oakland, but he took me west, and he charged me more.

I was supposed to stay with my brother Willie. He lived out by River Rouge, but I didn't want to live out there so I stayed with my Uncle Jamie Ware in the city. I stayed there six months and I looked for jobs, but I didn't find any. I was drawing unemployment from Alabama, fifteen dollars every week. Big money! They transferred it up to Detroit, and I went to the unemployment office there, and they took care of it.

When I first came up, I was babysitting. My Uncle Jamie had a little girl. His lady was working, and he was working. His lady would go to work around one o'clock in the afternoon, and he didn't get home until three thirty, so I would watch the baby those couple of hours.

Sometimes he would put stuff on me, "Hey, would you keep the baby for an hour, I won't be gone but about an hour. I want to go and shoot some dice."

"OK, an hour."

Sometimes he would be back in an hour, most of the time he wasn't. So I used to keep the girl about every day. The baby was about five or six months old when I came up to Detroit.

I MET THIS GUY, Walter Frank King. He was living not too far from my uncle over in the North End. He was born in Detroit, but I found out his mother grew up in Alabama.

Walter showed me a paper that said he was the leader of a gang, but his mother told me he was lying about that, "He wasn't no leader of that gang. He was just fourteen or fifteen. The leader of that gang was in his twenties." Walter was in the younger group. They were the ones doing most of the crazy stuff. The older guys told them what to do, and the younger ones wanted to be in the gang so they did it, any crazy shit the older ones told them to do. The young ones are the most dangerous ones because they don't care, just do whatever the older ones tell them. And Walter was like that.

But when I met him, the gang thing was already over.

I went with him and his friends to this theater on Woodward, just past Grand Boulevard. We used to sneak into the movie there. Four or five of us together would be hanging out. I had my fifteen dollars a week unemployment coming from the ice cream company. So I had pocket money every week. I would pay, and one of the guys would go in with me. I might loan him a dollar. Then this guy would go down to the back of the theater where they had a side door, and he'd open the door when the Security was at the other end. The rest of them would be there waiting on him to open that door. They would sneak in and crawl on the floor. The Security would see that door open, but by the time he got over that way, they had sneaked up the aisle the other way and took a seat. He could close the door but he wouldn't know who came in. Later on, the others would find out where we were, and they would come over and we would sit together.

They took me places on the bus, different places. We went down in the Black Bottom. There was always stuff going on down there. They would take me down to Hastings Street. I would pay and maybe one more guy with me, we would pay to get on the bus. We stood right up there by the bus driver, and while we were paying, a couple more would ease right on past, back of us. Gone just like that—they went right on back and sat down. We would go back and sit down. We didn't say anything to any of them.

They always had this kind of scheme going on. They'd been doing it. That was them.

One time, we went to a Teen-Time dance—me, Walter, Earl, and this young boy whose name I forget. It was right on Clay off of Oakland, on the East Side of Detroit. That's where most black people lived. Some, a few, may have already moved on the West Side. There was a junior high school on the West Side, where black students had begun to go. But most didn't live west of Woodward at the time.

Walter was talking to a girl. Some guy—maybe she was his girl friend, I don't know—anyway he got into it with Walter. He and Walter got to duking it out. Then another guy came up behind Walter and grabbed him, punched him in the back of the neck. The first guy hit Walter in the eye.

When they did that, I grabbed the second guy and pulled him off of Walter. About that time another guy came up behind me and hollered "Freeze," like he had a gun or a knife. I heard a click. May have been a knife. Walter and this first dude kept on swinging, but the Security came over and put us out.

By the time we got out, Walter looked on the side of the building and saw some bottles there. He grabbed some and broke them. He held them like a knife, like he was going to cut someone. Told them, "Come on, I'll run through all you motherfuckers. Y'all don't know who you fuckin' with."

Walter and me were about eighteen. Earl was about seventeen at the time, and the other boy who was with us was about fifteen. The other guys were fifteen, sixteen, maybe seventeen, but there were five or six of them. Earl got scared, and he took off. That made Walter mad. "Motherfucker run off and leave us." The three of us were left, facing five or six guys. Still when Walter came out and started talking shit with those bottles, "Come on," they didn't come on. They just stood there.

So finally we just left.

Walter came by the house the next day and said "Let's go."

"Where you going, man?"

"Going nigger hunting."

Walter was still mad. His eye was swollen where the guy had punched him. Walter was pissed off because his eye was a little swollen. Yep, that was Walter. He wanted to get that guy who'd hit him in the eye.

All those young guys went to Northern High School. So we went there, stood out on the sidewalk on the corner of Woodward and Owen. There used to be a little hang-out place there. The guy Walter was waiting on never did come out. I think somebody had hipped him that we were out on the corner. He didn't come out, so Walter didn't get him.

One time, I was with Walter, we went down to the skating rink. That was on Woodward near the movie theater. He was about to hit a girl because of something she said to him, grabbed her skate from her and was fixing to hit her with her own skate.

I checked him, "Walter! Naw, don't hit the girl, man." He just stopped. Probably he was reading me.

After I left Detroit the first time, I saw Walter again a couple of times. In 1959, I went by his house and visited him. Later on in 1962, I came through Detroit from L.A. I met his mother and his youngest brother. And I think I ran into him at the unemployment office. Walter had been sick and wasn't doing too good. I think he died not too long after that.

I NEVER DID get a job in Detroit that first time. I went places looking, but at that time period, 1958, it was real down. My brother Willie tried to get me on at a place he was working. He was working for a guy who ran some kind of store. He worked for them a long time. Even after he went to work at a parts plant, he worked for them part time. But they weren't hiring anyone. I went to work with one of my older cousins Clarence Ware, just little part-time stuff, doing a little painting. But I didn't find a job.

I WENT BACK DOWN to Bessemer, the last part of June in 1958.

My daddy passed the same month I got back. He died early. I think he was forty or forty-one when he died.

I didn't know he was dying. He'd had a problem with his throat for a long time, but he didn't go see a doctor. He got cancer in his throat, and it spread. Plus he was already having a problem with his prostate—you know, how men have to go to the bathroom all the time. He'd had a problem with that for quite some time. He finally went to the hospital, and they did some surgery on him, but they said the cancer had spread throughout his body. He was in the hospital just for a few days before he died.

I think I may have seen him smoking when there was a crowd around, take a cigarette or two. But my daddy never really was a smoker. But he worked on those jobs with all that pollution.

He worked one of the highest paying jobs in Bessemer, at Pullman. Just like working in auto, it was a big industry. But my daddy was bringing home only seventy-some, eighty dollars a week. Ma'Dear was making more selling Moonshine. I remember I used to take his pay check for him to get it cashed somewhere. I saw the receipts. I know it was eighty dollars and some. After they got through cutting it, after they took out taxes, it wouldn't be a hundred dollars.

Back in the early 1950s, he was making less than a hundred dollars. Not much over two dollars an hour. And all that pollution.

Before my daddy died, he had three other kids with two other women.

When he died, my mother signed some papers to help a woman who had two of those kids. She said, "These kids got nothing to do with what it is." She was looking at it from the kids' point of view. "Daddy's gone. The kids got nothing. If they can get something from him dying, then so be it. They had nothing to do with what their daddy did." My mother signed papers so they could get something, some kind of money, had to be Social Security.

My mother could have said, "I'm married to him and they ain't mine." She could have fought it. But she said, "Let those kids have it." I remember that too. I know a lot of people wouldn't have done that. But she was looking out for the kids. You can't go against them for what their father did. My mother was like that, she was a person like that.

SO I WAS BACK DOWN in Alabama and back to work at Superior Ice Cream in the summer of 1958. I worked there for another year and something.

It seemed like I was always having problems with the cops. One time, they stopped me and my brother Ocie the same night. "Yeah, we just stopped your brother tonight"— that's what he told me.

Ocie was driving another car then but I was driving the Cadillac. When my daddy passed, my mother didn't drive, so we drove his Cadillac, just like it was our car. So the cops saw that. They didn't like it.

I WAS LEAVING my girl friend's house, walking home. It was about a mile. I was just four blocks from my house, when the cops drove by me. They stopped me.

They asked me, "Where you been?"

"At my girl's house."

"Where you going?"

"I'm going home."

"Did you break into that white woman's house?"

"No, I was walking the whole time after I left my girl's house."

After I told them what time I left, they put me in the car and drove over to my girl's house. She told them that she didn't know what time it was.

But when they came out, one of them said, "Well, the girl said you left there at such and such a time. If you left there then, you should have been home by then."

I didn't have a watch on. But I knew what time I left. I told them, "When I got down there at 8th Avenue, the lights was already out." The traffic lights went out in Bessemer at a set time. "Maybe she didn't know what time it was. But I know what time I left."

They took me to jail anyway. A cop inside was asking me questions. I guess he was reading me. Anyway, he let me go. I had to walk home, nearly another mile.

Sam and his younger brother, Ocie, 1958

I STARTED thinking about going to California. My uncle
Jamie Ware had already called, telling us to come out there.
That was my mother's youngest brother. He went out there
from Detroit at the beginning of 1959, the first of the family
to go to California.

I was talking to one guy, Mayfield—the man I went to
jail with—I was talking to him about California. One guy at
work heard us talking. That was Peg. He had a wooden stick
he balanced on because his leg was cut off right above the
knee.

When I went in and tried to borrow some money from
one of the bosses, this little Peg had already told them,
"Don't you let him have it, 'cause I heard him, he's going to
California." We called him Uncle Tom after that.

The boss told me right out, "I hear you're going to
California, that's why you're trying to get the money."

But I was talking about going later, I had already set
the time when I was planning on going, at the end of 1959.
I wanted the money then because there was something I
wanted to do. But this sucker went in and told the boss. So
the boss didn't let me have the money.

ONE DAY, this young white guy went out to lunch. Poor
white. He'd been drinking. When he came back, he brought
the bottle back to give us a taste. He had it in a bag. He put it
in the cold storage where they kept the ice cream. He stashed
it in there. A supervisor—one of the owner's cousins—went
right in behind him, saw what he put in there, carried the bag
out, holding it up. The owner smelled the liquor on him and
gave him the rest of the day off. He got busted and we never
did get a drink.

On lunch time we'd talk. He liked the music we were
listening to, Little Richard and Chuck Berry and some Blues
singers, Howlin' Wolf, Bobby Blue Bland. A couple times,
he said, "Man, I'd like to go out, hang with you guys."

I said, "I would like to, but you know it would be a problem. If we go anywhere together at night, it's a problem." I knew definitely I couldn't go to a white place with him. And even if I took him to a black place, there could be a problem.

I WOUND UP going back to Detroit early in 1959 and stayed about a month. My oldest brother Willie was in an accident in Detroit, and almost paralyzed for a while. He busted his head, had a plate in it. And he had a cast from his neck all the way down to his waist and kept that cast on a month or two. Ma'Dear was going up and she wanted me to go with her. I knew the city, and she knew she wouldn't have to be worried about getting lost if she had me with her. And I was laid off again. We stayed about a month, a little over a month until Willie came out of the hospital.

He couldn't talk. It messed up his senses, he couldn't smell, couldn't feel and had no taste. He could understand what people said, but he couldn't talk. The doctors said he was going to come back. They had that problem before, I guess. He got in the habit of writing little notes when somebody would say something to him because he couldn't speak. When he got out, things started to come back, but it took a while for him to get his taste back. Food didn't have any taste for him.

When he got up and started moving around, my mother and I went back to Alabama. I stayed around for the rest of 1959, and went back to work at Superior.

TWICE WE TALKED about going to California—my brother Ocie, my cousin Carlos, who was the son of my mother's sister Patience, plus a friend Big Sonny, and me. But something came up and we put it off. Finally, in December 1959 we were supposed to go.

We were sitting there, in the house, talking. Ocie and Carlos said they were ready. But I didn't have the money. I told them to go on, I wasn't ready to go.

Sadie B. heard us talking, and she said, "Unh-uh. No. You go. You take this money and you go now." She wanted me to leave. She didn't want Ocie going out there alone, only with Carlos. She gave me $40.

She was thinking about all the things I had been into with the cops since I was seventeen. And just ten miles away in Birmingham, they killed three young boys just before I left Bessemer.

Sadie B. said, "Them boys ain't hardly did nothing. They just spoke out and said something, that's it. The KKK and police killed those boys."

My mother saw that. And she knew me. The police were stopping me, coming by the house. She knew if they came at me, I wasn't going to just lay down. I spoke out, and when you do that, they're coming after you, the lynchers, the KKK, and a lot of the KKK were cops.

We left for California, January 1960. I was twenty.

After I was gone awhile, my mother said the cops came by, asking "Where's Sam?"

"Why? What you want him for?"

"Ain't no problem, just haven't saw him. Wanted to know if he was still here."

"No, he's not here. Why you want to know now? When he was here, you was messing with him."

Part Two
California, 1960-1967

Ten
To Los Angeles and Back

WE DIDN'T MAKE IT out to Los Angeles right away. Four of us, Ocie, Carlos, Big Sonny and me, we first went in the wrong direction to Houston, Texas. We didn't know where we were going, never been out there before. Then we had to have a tire fixed. This guy in Texas fixed it—supposed to have fixed it, but we got two blocks away and the tire was going bump, bump. We went back to the guy, got another tire from him, and paid for that and for some gas.

Big Sonny came back and said, "Man, this guy wants us to pay him again for putting the tire on."

I asked him, "Did you pay him?"

"No."

"So fuck him then."

We took off. How are you going to put us back on the road and you ain't fixed the tire, and then charge us again for not fixing it in the first place? This is what pissed us off.

He had said sure he could fix it, but he was kind of cold and acted like he really didn't want to fix it. Like a lot of whites, he had an attitude from the beginning.

That guy called the cops. They picked us up about one or two in the morning. We had to stop in another gas station for the car overheating. The cops were waiting right there. The white guy who had fixed the tire told the cops a lie. He said we had filled up a tank of gas and then didn't pay. I told the police officer what had happened, that the guy tried to charge us twice for fixing the tire. The guy finally admitted to the detectives it was a tire problem. But they took us to jail anyway. Detectives came in and checked us out. Was the car stolen? Were we wanted some place else? Did we have arrest warrants out for us any place?

Finally, they let us go about six or seven in the morning. One of the cops tried to make a joke, "Well, maybe you guys got a good, long rest break."

"Yeah, well, maybe we did," we said. And we left.

We were trying to get to a highway to Los Angeles, but we went out of our way, about three hundred miles south toward Houston out of our way, before we got straightened around. We finally made it to Los Angeles but we were on the road much longer than we should have been, about three days.

On our way to L.A., we picked up a young white guy, maybe, if I'm not mistaken, just before we got out of Alabama. We gave him a ride, and he went to Texas with us. In Texas, my cousin Carlos said, "I had some extra money, but I can't find it now," trying to make it look like the young white guy took the money. It was a lie. We had all agreed we would put in so much money each for the trip. After we got in L.A., Carlos admitted he didn't ever have that money.

Anyway, we stopped at a restaurant, but we couldn't go in. This was in Texas, not Alabama or Louisiana, but in Texas. All those places were still like that, segregated. It wasn't until 1965 or '66 that most of that began to change. So this young white guy went in to get us some food. But he was worried that we would think he really took the money. So when he brought us back our food, like he said he would, he said they had offered him a job in the restaurant, so he was going to stick around there for a while. He said, "Thank you for the ride." And we went on.

WE WERE SUPPOSED to find my uncle Jamie Ware when we got to California, but he moved, and we didn't know where he moved to. We wound up staying at Arnold Moore's place. He was Carlos's cousin on his daddy's side. We were there over a week until my uncle came to find us. Jamie had finally called back to Alabama to ask what happened to us.

Carlos and Ocie got a job right away at a car wash on Manchester. But they didn't last there but a minute. Instead of Ocie doing his job, he was out there doing his own car! So the man fired him. We went out to Rancho car wash, and they got a regular job. I was working just weekends part-time at first. Then I finally got full time.

We moved around a few times. Then we moved into an apartment building with a family that was from Alabama, Carlos and me. We knew these people. My mother and the woman used to work together at the chicken place. Her son was the manager of the building. So we had no problem getting an apartment there. It was close to our job at Rancho, on Pico between Hollywood and Santa Monica.

The owner of the car wash was from England. The manager was a black guy from Oklahoma, and his cousin was assistant manager. We used to ride with the cousin to work.

There was a guy from Louisiana. He said he thought that all of them from Louisiana were crazy, "but y'all from Alabama are crazier than us!" We used to be cutting up all the time, didn't give a hoot. We'd be out late drinking, come in, cut up on the line, just like that movie, *Car Wash*.

One day, three of us bought some liquor. I just got one taste of it, then I went back to cleaning the car, detailing it, checking it out. I went back to get me another taste, but I didn't see the other two guys any more. The manager had cut their time for the day, he didn't need them. So they laid down in their car getting high and fell asleep. But I didn't know that. I thought they were in the bathroom. I knocked on the door. "If y'all don't open it, when I come back, I'll kick it in and get my part." I went and detailed a few more cars and then came back and knocked. But no answer, so I kicked it in. But it was empty. I went back to the job.

The manager came around looking at everybody's shoes, looking to see whose print was on the door kicked in. He came back to me and said, "You kicked the door in, nobody has shoes like that but you."

"Oh, since you such a smart investigator, okay detective, did you check those three, four hundred customers that came through here? How you know they didn't do it?"

He gave me the rest of the day off, but then he came and talked to me about repairing the door. I told him the bathroom door was locked and I had to go, that's why I did it. He said he would pick up the strips, and all I had to do was pay for the strips, he would put it back together. So I agreed, and that is the way we worked it out. The manager had to have some story to tell the owner, but he was OK. And his cousin, the assistant manager, would pick us up in the morning like always. His cousin was older than us, but we were always tight. We used to give him something on gas, and he'd pick us up. He was in the Second World War in Europe, and he told us he stayed around in Europe for some years before he came back.

AFTER ABOUT NINE MONTHS, maybe September or October of 1960, I went back home. I came home just about every year to visit Sadie B. and the rest of the family, went around to see all those family and friends. We knew a lot of people.

I was going to ride back with Johnny Balwin, someone I knew from Jonesboro, knew him since grade school, and a guy named Levi. They were both working at Rancho car wash. Those guys didn't stay in L.A. too long, less than a year, then they went back to Alabama to stay. Johnny Balwin rebuilt engines for hot rod cars. He had put a '56 engine in his '52 Chevrolet. That's what we were going to drive back. Johnny Balwin had raced a couple of guys in his car, but they beat him. So he said he had to rebuild his engine again before we could leave. He rebuilt that engine up in the apartment building at night, the same building we stayed in. Put in more pistons and built that engine up to make it more powerful. After he did that, he got this kid lived upstairs and me, and we carried it down the stairs. He made a pulley and a chain thing that would raise the engine up, so he could drop it back in his car. We finally got it back in his car, went out there burning rubber and acting crazy. All he said was, "It's ready, guess I got to get some more tires." The tires couldn't deal with the power he had, couldn't get traction.

When he got back to Alabama, he got him a shop, building engines for other guys, plus he would build hot rod cars, take them to the racetrack. He was into that. Back in Bessemer, he had that engine shop right up off 8th Avenue and 24th Street.

WE RAN INTO LITTLE RICHARD in Texas on our way back to Alabama. He saw our Alabama license plates and he honked his horn at us. We stopped to see who it was.

"Don't you guys know me? I used to perform all around through Alabama."

"Oh, yeah, Little Richard."

He was from Georgia, but when he first started singing, he would be all around in Alabama, in Birmingham, or in Bessemer at the old theater where blacks could go. In 1960, when we saw him on the road, he had stopped singing. He had started preaching, preaching out in Texas. He took us out to lunch. He talked to one of the guys, Sammy, and talked him into staying down there. Sammy didn't have to worry, Little Richard would get him home. And so Sammy stayed on down there for three days or so. We had heard then that

Little Richard was gay.

While we were in Texas, Little Richard took us into this white restaurant to eat, everything was cool. He paid for everything. Then he left. We tried to go right across the street to get a beer. We were standing there at the bar, but the woman behind the bar kept moving around. She wouldn't come and see what we wanted.

She finally did come over, "What you guys want?"

We told her we wanted a beer.

"Well, you know, I can sell you a beer, but you can't drink it in here."

It was just like Alabama, racist, prejudiced, segregated.

We went to another place in Texas, came in the front, and they took us right on back where they cook at, and they put us at a table back there. We were used to that, just the way it was, nothing new. We thought maybe it could be a little different in Texas, but it was the same thing.

Eleven
Hanging with the Fast Crowd

I WAS HANGING with the fast crowd back in L.A. One night in 1961, I had a fight with George Moore, a cousin of my cousin Carlos. That's when I got these cuts on my face. They were all going to Tijuana to hang out one night. They asked me to go.

"No, I don't have any money."

"Come on, we'll take care of you, don't worry about it."

So I went on with them, six of us, in George's station wagon. George, his wife Clarice, my sister-in-law N.E., a friend of George's, and my lady friend, Lorine, and me. We were high as a kite, taking pills and drinking liquor. Tequila and something else, I forget what. We were crazy, throwing the empty bottles out the window, drinking up all the liquor we had in the car on the way back to George's brother's house. He was having a party.

Time we got back, Arnold Moore and his girl friend were having it out. She came running out of the house. I walked up, said, "Hey come on back, we came here to party."

Then Lorine started to act up, accusing me that I had something going with Arnold's lady. She slapped me, and I grabbed her, slapped her back and pushed her back out of the way. Then George Moore tried to tell me I shouldn't hit her. But what I saw, she was acting crazy and hit me first. I told him, "Hey, that's my woman, not yours."

He started to grab me. We started tussling, and I flipped him and had him down on the ground, beating him. He got up and ran back to his station wagon. He got his knife, a work knife. My brother Jesse had sharpened it for him.

I didn't see him, I had my back to him, going in the house, thinking it was over. His brother Arnold saw him coming and tried to stop him. George cut his own brother first, on the leg right up through the groin, he was that out of it. He came up behind me and grabbed me, snatched my arm around. I started swinging at him right away, I didn't know he had a knife. He cut me three times before I even saw he had a knife. Cut me on the side of the face, down my eyebrow and in the head, along my ear and my jaw, and on my hand. Then I fell and he got on top of me and swung that knife. Both my hands got cut because I tried to grab that knife and take it away from him. It wasn't a stabbing-type knife. It was more square, like a box-cutting knife. I almost got it from him, I was hanging on to it so tight. Finally he got it back, but about then the police got there. Somebody had called them because of all the noise. They came up and got him off me and arrested him and took me and his brother to the hospital. I was bleeding like crazy, cut in the head all over, side of the face, about five times. His brother had twelve clamp-like stitches or staples on his leg where he got cut.

After he got out of jail, George came around, wanting to apologize. My cousins Frank Ware and Carlos were mad at him. Carlos and I were real close. I was like a big brother to them. I would run to the bars with them. I was two years older, so I was their lead man. Frank kept asking me when I wanted to go get him.

But I said, "Fuck it, just let it go." I knew we were all out of control with the pills and drink. He was and I know I was, and I probably hurt his ego a little. He was three or four years older than me. Plus I knew I would end up in jail if I did go after him. So I just let it go, and he came over and apologized. I didn't press charges, and the police let him go. I'd been knowing George ever since I was growing up in Alabama. The Moores were like family, cousins to some of my cousins. His brother Arnold got hurt trying to stop him from cutting me. When I had time to think, why am I going to do something against him?

GEORGE GOT ME A JOB with the janitor service he was working with, a night job. This company had contracts with different places, so I worked all over the place, at air traffic control out at Santa Monica, at computer places, I forget them all, just north of Hollywood and in Pasadena. I worked out by the desert, cleaning the offices at TRW, the company that built technology for planes for the military. The same week, maybe we worked at two, three different places. Then I worked with George's brother Arnold, cleaning at a little shopping center in the Valley, about twenty miles north of where I was living in L.A.

One of the guys working there was from Mississippi. He was the lead guy, got there before we started. That guy was always saying to us, "Be careful, don't put your hands on nothing, they got them eyes all over. Don't try to take nothing."

We had eight hours to do the work, but we got so used to doing it, we did it so fast, we could get it done in four. Sometimes one of us would do the work, the other two would go out, hang out somewhere until one or two o'clock then come in. But we got the work done. We would go back in the cafeteria, get food we wanted for lunch, leftover cooked chicken or whatever. We'd go in the supermarket in that mall, get lunch meat and bread.

We used to watch TV a couple hours. They had workout things—exercise machines, bikes, other things—and we would use it all. Watch late movies, we didn't get off until six thirty in the morning.

One night, I was on my break, watching TV, and Arnold went running over to the market to get something to eat. He was trying to get in before the stock guys came. The security guard was up above, watching us. He saw Arnold running, and he moved and knocked over something. I heard the noise and called Arnold, told him, "It sounds like somebody upstairs."

Arnold and the guy from Mississippi went up to see what made that noise. They found this white security guard, told him to come out from there. "What you doing? You watching us?"

He said, "No, no, no," said he wasn't watching us, said he was watching the supermarket guys. He was watching us, but I guess he was scared to say it to our face.

They had some Mexican guys working there. We would race around on the shopping carts. One time, I was racing with one of the Mexican guys and hit the cashier booth partition, tore it all down. I didn't say anything, but the Mexican guy told them, said it was me and Arnold.

One night, I happened to go into the bathroom. The lead guy from Mississippi had his pants down and shirts wrapped all around his legs, four shirts, taped down, and one on under his regular shirt. So that's five, plus another pair of pants on under his regular pants! He just looked a little bigger. I walked in and said, "What are you doing?" "Oh, nothing I just got me some stuff. Y'all can go get you some stuff too." That was the same guy who told us not to take nothing.

WE WERE AT THE ALL NATION BAR on Broadway about 84th Street in L.A., a few blocks from Manchester, on a Friday night in April of 1962. Somebody came by and said the cops had gone in and shot up the Muslim temple. The temple was at 54th Street and Broadway, about three miles north of the All Nation. I used to live on 45th, one block west of Broadway, not too far from that temple. The cops killed one person, and I think they wounded six or seven others, and one guy wound up paralyzed.

After the temple was shot up, Malcolm X was talking about organizing Muslims from across the country, coming out to face down the L.A. police department. This is probably when Elijah Muhammad decided to push Malcolm out. I already had some contact with Muslims out there then, but they didn't ever talk about Malcolm. I didn't hear about Malcolm until I came out to Detroit. About a year and a half after the shooting, Malcolm was suspended when he made that statement about "chickens coming home to roost" after Kennedy was assassinated. And Malcolm started to build up his own organization. I'm quite sure there were Muslims that stayed with Malcolm out in Los Angeles but I was never in contact with those Muslims. At that time I didn't know about any of that.

But when the cops shot up the temple, I was down there on Broadway about three miles from where the temple was. I heard more about it the next day, people really talking about cops shooting the place up.

RIGHT AFTER THE SHOOT-OUT in the Muslim temple, I was stopped by the cops. A friend of mine was driving my car because I didn't have my license with me. Some guys were trying to get a ride, and they came across the street and wanted to know were we going north, could we give them a ride. As soon as these guys got in the car, the cops pulled us over and searched the car. They found a knife down in the back seat, but since it was my car it was supposed to be my knife.

Probably it was one of those guys we picked up who stuck it there. But I said, "I don't know what's in the back seat, I just bought this car, I never had that seat open. That knife could have been in there when I bought it."

"It's your car, so it's your knife."

The cops took me and my friend who was driving to the Tenth Precinct. That was my first time in the Tenth Precinct.

My man was talking to them, telling them, "What you want to do this for, I make more money than you do."

They didn't like the way he was talking, so they put us in the round-up, trying to find something on us. Finally, they let us out, didn't charge us with anything. Just harassment.

I had already noticed, any time more than two of us were out in a car, they would definitely pull us over. Just like that. You ain't did nothing, but they were checking you out. They stop you for nothing, then they run your name through the system, trying to find a ticket or a warrant or something else to put on you.

I WAS WITH SOME GUYS from Alabama, two I didn't know before, but met in L.A. We got in a car and went down Manchester from the All Nation Bar. We made a right and here come the cops. I don't know where they came from, but there they were, right along beside us, looking in the damn car. So we went on down toward Hoover, fixing to go north to drop somebody off. We got to Hoover, we made a right and the cops went across into a service station and got right behind us and pulled us over. Just like that.

"Get out of the car."

We hadn't done nothing. We had just left the bar. The guy who was driving, he didn't drink that much. We'd all had something but he hadn't. Didn't have time to do anything.

I asked them, "Why you pull us over? I know my friend driving didn't make any bad driving act. Did you pull us over because you saw four black faces in the car?"

"We can pull you over for suspicion or anything."

I said, "For anything? For nothing? Just messing with us?"

He didn't like the way I was talking. So he patted me down, and I had a knife in my pocket. He pulled out that big switchblade knife, and said, "Didn't you know this knife is illegal?"

"Illegal? I just was stopped last week and the officer didn't say anything, he gave the knife right back to me." That was a lie.

"Well, this is illegal, over three and a half inches long." He asked me, "Have you ever been to the Tenth Precinct?"

I had, but I told him no.

"Well, you ask someone what we do to smart ones like you." Just like that, smart ones like me.

So I asked him, "Are you from Alabama?"

"No, I was born and raised right here in L.A."

"Reason I asked you, when I left Alabama, I thought I was getting away from all that—all I was going through in Alabama."

I think that kind of backed him off a little bit. He took the knife and opened the trunk of the car and threw it into the trunk. He started trying to act like he wasn't prejudiced or anything. He didn't write a ticket, and they let us go. So we went on.

Twelve
To Alabama and Back to L.A.

I WAS HANGING OUT and I came in late to work one night. Someone had punched me in, but the security watched me coming in. So I got fired. They said it was like stealing.

So I wasn't working. I went back to Alabama with two of my cousins and my young uncle, stayed for three months and more in 1962. We came from L.A., went to Chicago, spent a night or two in Chicago with one of our cousins, then went to Detroit. My uncle got married to the lady he had been living with and had a daughter with. A week or so after that, we headed out from Detroit going to Alabama.

Ocie was already back there. My sister-in-law Grace had got pregnant again, and they went back together. When we got to Alabama, my brother Ocie talked me into staying for a couple weeks, so he could get his car fixed, and I'd help him drive back to L.A.

Ocie's car was still in the shop, and that went on for over two months. I got to thinking I was back home to stay then.

I STAYED WITH MY MOTHER. Sadie B. was very active, had her plants and things. She had her garden in the back, okras, collard greens, tomatoes, a few stalks of corn. That was some work to keep that garden going. And she had trees with peaches in the front and the back. She had flowers in the front, and those elephant leaves.

96

She and her sisters all grew up on the farm. They were used to working hard.

By that time, all of Sadie's sisters were living around Bessemer—except for her youngest sister, Delores, who was already up in Detroit. My aunts Clara Mae, Bea and Tulla all lived in Bessemer, right near where Sadie B. lived. My grandfather and grandmother were living with Clara Mae. Then there was Aunt Patience living out south of Birmingham, along with Lillie, Ann and Lou. Sadie B.'s oldest brother, William, had been killed in a workplace accident, electrocuted, a long time before. Henry, her next oldest brother, was living in Bessemer, Elbert was living in Tuscaloosa and Charlie was living in Hueytown. Her youngest brother, Jamie, was out in L.A.

Sadie B. wasn't doing parties any more. But she had money coming in all the time. She was still working. And people still came through, got something to drink. That was all the time. She had a certain number of people, they definitely would come. They'd bring someone with them. The new ones would get to know her, so they'd come too. The ones who knew her might not pay right then. They would come by, get a shot or a half pint, pay later. Then they came by and paid her on the weekend when they got their check.

By this time, Sadie B. was keeping a three-gallon jug out in the garden, down in the ground out near the creek. When she ran out of pints, she went out and filled bottles up. Didn't keep it in the house.

The police looked in the house. Never looked in the garden. They looked around the side of the house, under the house, but never back in the garden.

ONE DAY, I was shooting dice up on the street where I grew up, Tenth Avenue. One of my aunties had moved into our old house. We were shooting dice right across from the old house—me, my cousin Rob, some others. This young dude wasn't shooting dice and I wasn't, but we had a side bet. If the shooter gets points, you can win on it. But if you bet against him, and he gets points, you lost the bet, you've got to pay up. I bet against the shooter, but I called off the bet before the guy threw the dice. He came back a couple times and shot two-three different times, made the point.

This young dude was going to come back and say I owed him. I said, "I offed the bet. I said it two or three times, I offed the bet."

He went on talking, saying, "You just took that, huh? You took that!"

I guess he wanted to start something, just had to do something. He had his hand in his pocket, so I stood up too and put my hand in my pocket. I had a razor in my pocket.

This young dude kept on saying, "Oh you took that huh?"

"You wanna say I took that, huh? OK, I took it."

He had a gang of guys with him, four or five with him, tough guys, but they were all younger than me, teenagers, two, three years younger. One of these guys I knew because I'd hung out with his older brother when I was younger. I'd been going over to their place, riding bikes, shooting marbles and things. So they'd been knowing me.

My cousin Rob was saying, "Come on, Sam, let's go, let's go," and he grabbed me and pulled on my hand. My hand came out, and the razor came open and cut his hand.

I went out the door with my cousin. The young dude followed me out the door, still talking, trying to get something going. He wanted to cut me, that was what he had been into, cutting people. So we got outside, and he started talking stuff again, wouldn't let it go.

One of the guys with him let me know, said, "No, I ain't with him on this." Two or three of them stepped back. They didn't want to get in on it just because this guy wanted to get tough.

He kept on talking, so I just came right on out, "Man, let

me tell you something, I give junior flips like you lessons every day, come on then," just letting him know he doesn't know what I know, he doesn't know who he's messing with.

His boys, none of them tried to jump me. And he stepped back. So we just went on and left him hanging there.

OCIE AND GRACE'S second oldest daughter was born while I was in Alabama that time. We call her Fay, but her name's Laquita. She was born November 1962. I went with Ocie to take Grace to the hospital. I once told Fay I was in the car when she almost came—it was about ten to twelve miles from Bessemer to Birmingham. That was where Grace had to go. It was a public hospital where you could go if you didn't have insurance. That's why we went that far.

FINALLY, OCIE GOT HIS CAR FIXED and we drove back on out to L.A.

Not long after I got back, my daughter Sammie Louise was born in January of 1963. The other kids started calling her Lulu.

IN THOSE YEARS, I was running high a lot of the time, drinking alcohol and taking "speed" too, those pills that keep you going. I know I was acting a little crazy sometimes and getting into fights.

Sometime in the year 1963, I had a fight with my brother Jesse. He was living over on Avalon. There was a party, and Clarice, the wife of George Moore, started talking shit. I forget how it actually started. But she brought that shit up about the fight George and I had. I was high and she pissed me off. I told her to shut up and started to raise hell with her. Jesse told me I had to leave, and he put me out. We got to tussling, my brother Jesse and me, fighting outside. I got him down. My cousin James Ware pulled me up, and Jesse went in the house and got his gun. He couldn't handle me the way he used to. I had got to that point, none of them could deal with me.

My cousin James didn't want anything else to happen. "Come on Sam, you're in his house. Just leave, just let it go."

My cousin James was three or four years older than me. He got through to me. I grew up around him, was used to listening to him. So I left.

I HAD IT OUT WITH my Uncle Jamie Ware, too. Carlos and me had been having a relationship with these two girls. We came over to their house. But the girls wouldn't open the door. My uncle and my cousin James Ware were in their house, acting like nobody was there.

I figured somebody was, "You might as well open, cause we ain't going nowhere, we will be right here until tomorrow." It was two or three o'clock in the morning, and they saw we weren't going anywhere, so they finally opened the door.

I got pissed off. We'd been up all night long. Here Uncle was messing around with one of the girls, when I was supposed to be in there. I must have slapped the girl up side her head, something like that. Uncle told me to cut it out, it wasn't our house. I was going to hit her again, but she ran behind Uncle. He said, "I told you to cut it out, if you don't stop you will have to come through me." So I wrestled him down on the floor, had him down, choking him.

My cousin James started talking to me, pulled me off him. "Cut it out Sam. Stop. You know you're family."

GROWING UP, it was like James Brown said, it's a man's world. A man's supposed to control his woman. That's what you're supposed to do. It's what I saw growing up, around my daddy and my uncles. That's what I saw. When kids grow up, their father or their uncle is the man of the house. They're right there, talking. You hear them. If you're going to be a man, then you're going to be like them. You just think that's how it's set up. And I grew up around that. But it's everywhere. Movies, TV, songs. Most men still think that way. In the 1970s, I was exposed to people with different ideas. I got a bigger picture. I was familiar with discrimination myself. I came to see that women were being treated like they are less than men. And I came to understand the system, and if you're going to change the system, you have to change that, too.

But back then I thought men were supposed to tell women what to do. You're the boss. You grow up being told, you're a man, you're not supposed to cry. What, crying? Are you a sissy? You're supposed to be hard. You don't shed no tears. For years, I never did. I guess you grow up and your body gets set that way.

Thirteen
The Nation of Islam and the Streets

THE KKK BLEW UP that church in Birmingham in 1963. They went in there and blew it up—a church, killed four young girls. The KKK had been doing stuff all along. But when they blew up that church, that was a big thing. It was four young girls.

I was in L.A. when that happened. I thought something should have been done—but who was going to do it?

In 1964, I began talking to some Muslim brothers on the streets in Los Angeles. I was living just one mile north of the Nation of Islam temple on Broadway and 54th Street. They were out there pretty regular, passing out flyers, inviting people to come to the temple, talking to people. The Black Muslims talked about building a black system for black people. They were blacks who stood together and were very militant.

Before I left California, I saw one young black woman working at the unemployment office. She asked me, "Why do you have your hair like that?"

I said, "I like it." I had it processed then, straightened in a "do."

I think she must have been a Muslim. She was the first somebody who said something like that to me, something to make me think about what I was doing. But we didn't get too much further. She didn't have any time to talk to me more because she was on the job.

Later on, a young Muslim in Detroit started talking to me about the same thing. He talked to me about how blacks don't like themselves, trying to be like a white person. "What's the matter, you don't like your own hair?" That's when I stopped wearing my "do." Then he and I started talking to another dude about the same thing.

But that was a couple years later.

In L.A., I talked to the Muslim brothers pretty regular. But I didn't go to the temple in L.A. because I was in the streets, smoking weed, taking drugs, drinking alcohol and hanging out with the fast crowd.

ONE NIGHT, I had just left the All Nation Bar, me and a guy named William Olds. We'd gone out to a party at someone's house nearby. We ran into these other Alabamas, Eddie Robinson and Kurt somebody. Then along came some guy, who had some other guys with him—he got into it with Olds. We didn't know those guys, didn't know what might go down. I got on the phone and called to the All Nation, just a few blocks away. Let them know, just in case something happened.

Some of my boys from the All Nation came over there. By that time, we were out of the party, outside, and those guys from the party were talking shit. One of my big guys from the All Nation came right up to me and asked, "Which ones?"

I took a quick look over at one of them. My big guy went right over to the dude and said, "You so and so, you messing with my man," and just hit him, just like that, Pow.

The rest of them, they were looking all shocked. What's going on? They didn't stay around to find out.

A month or so later, I was at a party with some of my same Alabamas, and up come three of those guys who had tried to jump my boy Olds. One of them said, "Yeah, he's the one that got on the phone and called them suckers over there." Those guys wanted to jump me. I had a fight with one of them in the rest room, wasn't bad. But after we came outside, two more of them jumped me. They had me down, kicking me.

That really pissed me off. I left and went over to find a friend of mine named Roy. I was trying to get a gun. This friend of Roy's had a .38, and he was going to let me have it. But Roy knew me, and he knew that I was too mad. Finally, Roy's friend said, "No man, I don't think I'm gonna let you have no gun."

So I went over to this girl's house. When I left out of there and headed to her house, I hit a post and tore it down. So she drove me back down there. She was crazy. I was high.

When we came back to where the party was, they were all gone. I knocked on the man's door and went on in.

He got pissed off, "Hey, why the fuck you in here?" My man, he was mad because I came back there. "Nigger, get the fuck out of my house."

"Man, I ain't come here looking for you, but if you gonna fuck with me, it could be you."

He went back in his room, I guess maybe to get a gun.

Another Alabama guy who knew me said, "Come on Sam, come on, come on man, let's go, let's get out of here." So I just went on out of the door. I got back in the car, and my girl took me on back to her house.

That wasn't the first time I was in something like that. The guy could have killed me or messed me up, or I could have killed him and ended up in prison. Probably something like that would have happened to me, sooner or later, if I hadn't started to get a bigger picture about what was going on. When you're out there doing things, when you're in the streets, you have to deal with people. If they come at you, you have to let them know you'll come back on them the same way. When you learn more about the world, you don't want to keep acting like that. But right then, that's how I was.

Fourteen
Watts, 1965

I WAS LAID OFF AGAIN and went back to Alabama with my brother Jesse in 1965.

On the way back to Alabama, we came through these small towns, Livingston and York, Alabama. People had signs, they were protesting. They wanted black girls and women be able to apply for cashier jobs. There was nothing for them. It always had to be a white person to do those jobs. The black women could only do cleaning in the stores. They had been to high school, they were qualified, but they couldn't get those cashier jobs. Most of the business in those stores came from blacks, too, because more blacks lived in those areas than whites. But black people couldn't get a "white person's job." It was like that all the years I came up in Alabama.

So young blacks were protesting down there, about a hundred and twenty five miles south of Birmingham. Protests had been going on in Birmingham, but I hadn't seen all of that. I was in California. So when I saw this protest, it was kind of like, "Wow, they're fighting." Those marches had a very important role in black history.

But I don't think I could have hung there very long. I couldn't hang with where Martin Luther King and them were coming from. I saw these guys lying on the ground, letting the racists beat on them. Unh-uh. Nah, I wasn't ready for that. I was for fighting back, turn it around. I couldn't go for the non-violence, that part of it. I wasn't for letting anyone beat on me. That was before I even knew about Malcolm X, about what he was talking about. It was just what I grew up on. That's why I respected the brothers from the Nation of Islam. They were somebody that stood up. They talked about fighting back.

WE GOT BACK to L.A. just before the riots jumped off. Things were getting real bad, the police harassing everyone. I was riding with this guy, down in Watts, right down by the precinct in Watts. They stopped us, three of us. It was during the daytime too, it was early. They pulled us over for some reason, I don't remember. But then they checked and my man owed a traffic ticket, so they busted us.

And then they said they had paper on somebody named Sam, the same first name as mine. The sergeant or somebody said, "Bring him on in, just bring him on in."

They tried to tie me to something happened over in Watts.

"Couldn't have been me. Must have been someone else. I don't even know the area. I never lived there, don't have family there."

"How long you been in California?" This went on for awhile.

They finally let me back out. But my man, they kept him. He left his car with us, but we didn't want to keep it, so we took it to his uncle. We knew him from the All Nation Bar. He was a numbers man.

THEN IT HAPPENED, August 1965, Watts.

My cousin Carlos came by and told me he had been down in Watts. That's where the revolt started, that's where they took down some mannequins from the store, dressed them with signs with different protests, and put them all in the streets.

106

Carlos had been in Watts, but then it started spreading, going north and east and west, spreading. This guy told me to come on over, "Just come on, they're going in the stores." It came up into the area where I was. I'm forgetting some of the streets now, Vermont, before you get to Crenshaw, I forget. Anyway, I was over there with this friend who took me on down there, not too far from where she lived.

They busted in a store, then everybody would go in. Most of what people got was just beer and wine. The first things people took when they broke into a store were cigarettes and liquor. That stuff would be gone just like that. What they didn't drink or smoke, they could sell. The wine and beer would be left; that went later. People went in other stores, took food, furniture. People needed things, they took anything they could carry away and get away with.

You could see the cops still moving around. They were standing around or driving by. I don't think any of them were standing right out front. But they were standing near and people were walking right in there, loaded up their baskets and walked right on out by them.

One woman had a little boy guarding a TV set until she could go get someone to help her. Some guy came up, trying to get the TV, and the little boy told him, "No, you can't get this one, it's my mother's TV. My mother said don't let nobody get this one." Just ten years old.

The guy said, "OK," and went on.

Fifteen
Working at Northrop, Leaving L.A.

I STARTED GOING TO SCHOOL in 1965, taking different classes, how to do wiring, stuff like that. They got me in through the unemployment office. But I never did get a job with what I learned.

After the classes, I went back to working janitor—what I'd been doing before. I was working at Northrop through a contractor, cleaning the building. That's when I met a young white guy, twenty or twenty-one. I went in there to do his room. He had a little office and he was running some kind of machine, pretty hi-tech. We'd be talking when I went through there cleaning.

One day, he asked me, "How come you're not working for the company?"

"I put in an application but they won't call me." When you're working someplace for a contractor, they make some kind of deal with the place, they won't hire you unless you quit and come back.

This guy told me, "I know some big timers around here, and I'm going to talk to them and see can I get you in."

A couple weeks later, I came in to clean his place and he told me, "I talked to someone, and when you get through, go down to Personnel, and put in an application. Tell them BabaJohn sent you." I don't know how it was spelled, but I've never forgot his name yet.

So I talked to a guy, I told him BabaJohn sent me down. He said, "BabaJohn?"

"Yeah. BabaJohn."

He said, "BabaJohn sent you down?"

"Yeah. Look, if you don't believe me, then you call BabaJohn." I didn't know it at first, but the young guy who sent me down to Personnel—that BabaJohn was his father.

So the guy in Personnel said, "Well, get over there and take these papers and fill these papers out." I was hired just like that. They had work that I knew how to do. I put it on my application that I had training in wiring, but they put me in paint. I was painting small parts.

I WAS TALKING TO ONE BLACK GUY who had worked at Northrop and then went to Viet Nam. He said before he left, he could count the black workers on his hands. When he came back, after the Watts riot in 1965, there were a lot more black guys working there. I guess the bosses figured they had to get blacks off the street, start putting them in heavy industry, give them jobs.

One day, one of the guys on the job was arguing with the little boss, saying he didn't want his son to go in that war.

The little boss called me and said, "Hey come here, what's wrong with him, he's a traitor to your race."

"Well, I'll tell you. I wouldn't go in that war either." And we were building the jet fighters that they used in Viet Nam. But we said we weren't for that war. I told him straight up, I wouldn't go.

The other guy hollered, "Before I let my son go over there in that war, I'll kill him myself."

I had heard Muhammad Ali talk about the war. He had refused to go in that war, and what he said made sense to me. That's why I already knew about it.

Sam's brother, Jessie, and his wife, N.E., and Sam with Sadie B. when she visited them in Los Angeles, 1966

THERE WAS ANOTHER GUY working right in my area. We used to sit and talk at lunch. He said he was part Indian, his mother was Indian, his father was white. When we got off work, he took me to this bar near the plant a couple times. This was in the suburbs.

One time, I was dancing out on the floor with one of the white girls. They hadn't had any blacks hang in there before, I guess. So it seemed like a lot of them were watching me. Maybe they were racist, maybe they were just watching to see the dance moves I had.

Another time, my friend was in the back playing pool. I was sitting up at the bar.

This white guy sitting right across from me, said, "What you doing in here?" With his nasty little attitude, asking me what I was doing there, like I wasn't supposed to be in there.

"What you mean, it's a public place isn't it?"

About then, my friend looked in, asked, "Is everything OK brother?"

"Oh, yeah, everything's OK."

"Well, if not, let me know, we'll turn this whole motherfucking place out."

That white guy across from me started talking then, trying to be friendly. He came way off the way he'd been talking before.

That young guy and me, we got to be close, talking at work and hanging out together. He liked to party and hang out. One night, I took him and some girls, some friends of his, over to my house and we sat around and played music. Another time, I took him to an after-hours place. He was the only white in there. I could see that some of the guys there were watching him. I told someone, "This guy's OK. He's one of my working partners. He's with me. Nothing to worry about." It's been so long, I forgot what his name was.

I BID ON A SET-UP JOB. A guy who was the set-up man took me on his job to train me. He was a teacher from New York and he was going back to New York. He had just begun to train me. But before I could get the job, I was fired. That was my last job out there. It didn't last no time because a security guard had that same old attitude. Security treated us different than they treated the whites. And I wasn't going for that shit.

One night, we were running late, we drove inside the gate to park so we could punch in on time. This guy I worked with was driving, but it was my car, I had rented it. He drove the car in past the security shack, and parked it.

It was my birthday, and I got a little high with a couple people working there. The supervisor was cool, he knew it was my birthday and asked me did I want an out pass. I said, sure.

I came out, and I walked out the gate—that's when it hit

me. The car was inside. I turned right around to get it.

But the white security guard said to me, "Where you think you're going?"

"To get my car."

He said, "Your car's not here."

I told him it was in there.

"Your fucking car's got no damn business in here."

I showed him my badge and said, "Look here, I work here, just like you do." I told him I was going to get my car.

That's when the shit started. He blocked me from walking back through the gate. That pushed me into the big water cooler, and it fell over. He said, "You, you're under the influence, you get in the shack."

I said to myself, "Oh, shit, this is it!" And it was it. I knew when a fight started I wasn't going to be there no more.

But I wasn't going to let him get away with that prejudice. He could just have written down my number, told my supervisor, let the supervisor deal with it. But, no, he had to act like he was the boss.

If that had been a white worker, he wouldn't have acted that way. That's what was pissing me off, and I was tired. "I'm not going in the shack, try and put me in the shack."

Another guard came up and hit me back of my head with his gun or flashlight. He must have knocked me out. The next thing I knew, cops had me by both legs, dragging me out to the street, my head going bump, bump, bump on the ground. I snatched my feet out of their hands, came up swinging on them. There were four of them, and they all kicked me and wrestled me down and put the handcuffs on me. It took all four of them to get me into the car.

That's when they started beating on me, saying, "Nigger, we're going to kill you!" They took me to jail.

That was 1967, March 17, my birthday.

I was in jail from Friday night to Monday morning. Then they took me to court in Inglewood. They took some of the charges off, just said I was under the influence and resisting arrest, and gave me a fine. I guess because the cops were doing some crazy stuff, they only charged me for "under the influence" and "resisting arrest."

I went back to work on Monday, and Northrop fired me.

OCIE WAS in Detroit then. He had already told me to come on. He was working at GM in Pontiac, Michigan. "They are hiring, come on."

I decided to go to Alabama, then Detroit. "I'm leaving L.A. I'm getting outta here."

It wound up I was in L.A. for another week and a half. I had to get some work done on the car. I didn't get to Alabama until the first part of April—on the bus, the car didn't make it. The frame was messed up. It was wearing the tires right on down. When I got it, I didn't know that. I drove eight hundred miles and had to buy two sets of tires for the front. I still had eleven hundred miles to go, and I knew I couldn't make it that way.

I got to El Paso and decided to leave the car, catch the bus. But I'd spent all my money trying to get the car fixed. I had to call my mother to get some change to catch the bus. I stayed for a couple days, waiting on the money. I stopped in a little old club. These guys playing in the band there told me they were from Alabama. They'd been going to California, but got stopped in El Paso by the cops and ended up in jail. After they came out, they never went to California, just stayed in El Paso.

One of the guys in the band was from San Antonio. I stayed for a couple of days, sleeping in my car in his driveway. He told me to wait until the weekend, "You could sell the car, man, to some of these soldiers. They come in on the weekend and just want something to ride around in. They don't care if it's messed up. They're not going far."

I gave him the car and the keys and the paperwork,

told him he could sell it, send me part of the money to my mother's house, keep the rest if he got anything.

I never did hear from him.

I stayed around Bessemer, two weeks with Ma'Dear in Alabama, before I left for Detroit.

When I was getting ready to take off, a friend of mine and his younger brother were driving to New York, headed to see their sister Dorothy and another sister Martha. Instead of going to Detroit, I drove to New York with them.

Martha tried to get me to stay there, "Why you going to Detroit, why don't you stay in New York?"

Dorothy's husband told me he had just gone through some training, and he said if I didn't have some training, it was going to be hard in New York. That was his problem before, he didn't have training, he couldn't get a job. "Detroit, man, where you going, it probably be better. You could go to the auto plants without training."

So I caught the bus and went to Detroit. I was twenty-eight years old.

Part Three
Detroit, Michigan

Sixteen
The 1967 Rebellion

I DIDN'T GET HIRED at General Motors when I first got to Detroit. My brother Ocie said they were hiring, but they were hiring mostly people who had been laid off and been out of a job in Detroit. My oldest brother Willie got me a job where he worked. I forget the name of the place, but it was a parts plant south of Jefferson on Woodbridge. I started as a press operator down there in May of 1967.

TWO MONTHS AFTER I got to Detroit, the riots jumped off around 12th Street and Clairmount. I was living with Ocie on 14th and Euclid, just a block west of 12th Street. Early that first morning, maybe about eight o'clock, I heard all this noise, people hollering and talking, and I came out on the porch. I saw one guy pushing a grocery basket and pulling one, full of groceries. Then, still, I could hear so much noise down on 12th Street, and I was a block away. I asked him, "What's going on?"

The guy said, "Well, you know, you better get on up there. It's free!" Just like that. "It's free! Get on up there!"

So I got ready and walked on up there to see what was going on. Police officers were standing out in front of the grocery store, and people were just walking right by them like they weren't there, going in and loading up their baskets and coming right back out. That was early in the morning on Sunday.

Later on in the day, I went over to my other brother Willie's house. He was living on Pallister behind Henry Ford Hospital. There was a store over there—they had looted that store, too. He went in to check it out, was gonna get him a drink or something. But all the liquor was gone!

That night or the next night, my brother Ocie rented a little trailer and had it full up with furniture and other stuff that he had snatched from somewhere. He was taking it on a trailer over to my oldest brother Willie's house. Willie had a garage out in his back yard. Before Ocie could get over there, the police officer stopped him and hollered, "Hey, you know it's after curfew!" Curfew was at nine p.m. You had to be off the street.

Ocie said, "Yes, I know, officer, but my house is burning now, and we had to get what we can get out of there."

"Okay, but you better get on, because you'll probably get stopped again."

Ocie'd been doing that for years, running something so smooth, so fast, that cop couldn't keep up with him! Yeah, that was Ocie.

I don't remember if that was the first night or the second night, but I know the second night the revolt was really spreading.

I remember Congressman John Conyers was up there on 12th Street, telling people, "We got to bring this to a halt, we got to stop this." That was Monday.

The young people that were there, most of them teenagers, yelled at him: "Uncle Tom, where was you when we needed you? We don't need you now." Boom! They started throwing rocks and bottles.

The car he was in, his chauffeur took off. I didn't even know who he was then. I was new. I didn't know who he was, but the young people knew. They were calling him out, "Uncle Tom! We don't need you now."

People were really going through all the stores. There was an incident when I was with my brother Willie. He wanted to get some furniture for his girl. "Might as well," he said, since people were taking, and they were burning those places down.

Before we could even get in the place, these guys come in and said, "Everybody out. We fixing to burn the motherfucker down!" Just like that.

I had to check him, "Hold on, man! Hold on! People need it. Why you gonna burn it up?"

"Okay, then, we going on. But when y'all get through, burn the motherfucker down." They just went on somewhere else. That's all they were doing, burning.

One of those places where there was looting, some people were in the basement and they got trapped by the fire. They died, I think. I don't know if somebody didn't know they were down there and threw a Molotov cocktail. It could have been some of those guys that were burning, didn't know anybody was down in the basement. If they threw a Molotov cocktail on the first floor, people could be trapped in the basement.

Some people had put signs up, "Burn, baby, burn!" on certain buildings and other things. Stores put signs up saying, "Black Owner." Some stores had blacks working there, I don't think many owned those stores at that time. They just worked there, acting like a little manager. They put up a sign so their place wouldn't get burnt down. "Black Owner." That's how they thought, "their place." But it didn't matter who owned them. People were burning the stores.

One night, right out in front of the house, a young guy, real young, was arguing with a police officer.

The police officer pushed him and said, "Get back, now."

He pushed the officer back and started yelling at him, "Motherfucker! You killed my brother! You killed my brother, motherfucker! Kill me then, motherfucker!"

Before the curfew, I was still moving around a little bit, walking about three blocks from where everything started at the blind pig the cops raided. The people in the streets were loud. That's why the police had been told, I guess, to just be calm. They figured then it would go quiet. But it just got bigger. It just got bigger.

On the second day, it spread all over to the East Side. On 12th Street, it went further north, up past Davison, and west at least up to Livernois.

South of Grand Boulevard, the streets were real solid white. Once you passed the Boulevard, between 14th back to 12th, all that part was mostly white. They were poor too. They were out there, taking things out of the stores along the Boulevard, and south of the Boulevard. You could see the whites out in the street too.

On the third day it spread some more. That's when they brought the troops in. Man, they had jeeps, with the M60 machine guns. They had tanks, going down the street. Coming down through 14th, there were troops with the tanks, and those troops shot out all the lights. The street lights! They shot them out! That seemed kind of crazy. Seemed like they could have turned them off. But they shot them all out. You know it made it dark.

I think that was when the troops shot up that building on Davison—it was a five or six-story building up there on Davison and 14th, an apartment building. That was crazy when they did stuff like that. They tried to say that somebody was sniping. Maybe someone was sniping. But they shot up the whole building.

That's the same thing they said, "someone sniping," when they shot and killed that three-year-old girl on Euclid. The father, all he did was sit in there, smoking a cigarette. They said they thought there was a sniper in there. They saw him light his cigarette and started shooting into the house and killed his little girl. That was right there on Euclid, two doors off 12th Street.

A laundry and cleaners was near where the little girl was shot; people in their little apartments lived on top of it. Somebody may have set the laundry on fire, burnt the apartment on top of it. The fire spread to the house next to it, and then spread to the house across the street from it. I guess the wind was blowing. I was up there, me and another guy I didn't know. There weren't hardly any firemen. We saw there were just two of them. With something like that they should have had four or five on that truck. But they only had two guys. They were pulling the line out, trying to hook it up, so we were helping them pull the doggone big lines and other stuff. So they got two people helping them right there. I was thinking, these people's houses don't need to burn. So anyway, we helped them. I think some guys over on Blaine were trying to help fight the fires. They knew. They were living right there.

I went over to my older brother Willie's house. At night, man, looking out the window I saw the troops all on the ground. Just like they talked about in Viet Nam, them suckers were crawling all around with their guns in their arms, crawling all around and looking. And you heard something like, "Pop!" That may have been the troops shooting. I don't know. But you couldn't see nothing. They were crawling all around with their guns in their hands just like they were in combat, in a war. Against us.

Another thing happened, it was on LaSalle, only about a block west of 14th. Some guys there did shoot, fired at the troops. Then the troops took that darn artillery and shot the whole place up, they shot it up! But those guys were in the basement. Then the troops yelled, "Anybody in that house?" They told them to come on out with their hands on their heads. So the guys came out. The troops thought they might have been black, but it was two white guys. It was two young white dudes. That was on LaSalle.

Then, there was that place over on Woodward, by Virginia Park. There was a motel there, the Algiers Motel. The Michigan National Guard was there, and private guards, and Detroit cops. They were mostly white, probably they were prejudiced. And they were ready to shoot at any little action. They saw one young black dude go inside the motel, him and this white girl. I think they might have beat them up first, but they wound up killing the young guy, then killed two other men inside the building. Executed all three of them. And they beat seven other young black men and two or three white women who were in the motel too.

I didn't go out to Belle Isle, but people said they had it roped off. I guess they had thousands of people out there. They had filled the jails. So they put people on Belle Isle, in the middle of the Detroit River. They weren't in jail, but they had the troops standing right there, and it was roped off. They couldn't get out. That was at Belle Isle.

I didn't know too many people that were locked down, because I didn't know that many people besides my family. I hadn't been here long. I would have had a bigger picture if I had been here for a while because I would have known people in different areas. You communicate, "Man, what's going on over there?"

But I didn't know many, so that's why I didn't know too much of what was going on. But I know one thing, people were coming in from cities in Illinois and Ohio, coming in from those states, grabbing stuff and taking it back. I know that was going on. I saw the doggone license plates when they were putting stuff in their cars. Especially Ohio and Illinois. A lot of those people from other states had families here, and they knew what was going on. People had contact.

It went on about five days. After the troops got here, it took them three days to bring things back under control. Well, it was a big thing. I think it was much bigger in Detroit than in Los Angeles.

I'VE BEEN THROUGH different things, been discriminated against and saw how the cops treated us. So to me, 1967 was a big thing. I really felt good. I saw that here all the cops in Detroit couldn't much deal with it. They couldn't deal with us. That's why they had to bring troops in, because they couldn't deal with us. So that makes you get a bigger picture. That's why I say if there are enough of us together, they can't deal with us. I saw that way back then. That's what really made me feel good.

Afterwards, they opened up places for people to put in applications for the auto companies. Right away. There was one right there on 12th Street—they changed the name afterwards to Rosa Parks—and Grand Boulevard. They set up a little office where they've got Martin Luther King Park now. You could put in an application right there for jobs at General Motors, Ford and Chrysler, all three of them. I guess they put that little office right in the neighborhood, so people could come right in to sign up. You didn't have to go to one of the plants. They did that to get those black people off the streets.

The auto plants went on hiring from 1967 until about '69 or '70. The corporations were thinking they had too many blacks in the street. They didn't want another riot—better give them jobs.

Later on, when I worked at the Big Three, I saw it: how few black people were hired before '67, and how many afterward. The big steel places too, they started hiring blacks—all because of the riots. Later on, when I was a union steward, I could look at the seniority lists and see it.

Seventeen
Working in Auto, Caught by Drugs

I WENT INTO the office on 12th Street, and I filled out an application, but I think they wouldn't hire me because I had just got to Detroit. I hadn't even been here three months.

So I stayed at the parts place. They made parts for Ford, General Motors and Chrysler.

A young Muslim guy was working there, and he started talking to me, talking about how blacks don't like themselves, trying to be like a white person. "Why you wear your hair like that? You don't like yourself?"

I was thinking about it after what he said. "Yeah, I like me." So, I stopped wearing my "do," just like that.

He and I started talking to another dude, younger than me, about the same thing. They were both younger than me.

I WAS RIDING TO WORK with an older neighbor when H. Rap Brown was on the radio, talking about Viet Nam. I heard him make his comment, "If anyone give me a gun and tell me to go shoot someone, I'll shoot the man give me the gun, 'cause I know he's my enemy." Then they cut him off fast. But he said it.

I said, "Whoa."

The guy I was riding with, he said, "What's wrong with that fool?"

"Don't sound like no fool to me." I had already heard

Muhammad Ali talk about the war before I came to Detroit from California.

Later on, maybe 1971 or '72, I heard about the war from my cousin, Junior. He served in Viet Nam. He had a relationship with a Vietnamese woman. She warned him about his friend who was in a bar, saying stuff like, "I'm thinking about killing me one of them Viet Cong." She told Junior he better tell his friend to shut his mouth before he got himself killed. She talked politics to my cousin. "Why are black soldiers over here fighting? Look at all the stuff you're going through back there, and you ain't fighting? You should be back there fighting."

When he came back, Junior was on heroin. A lot of the soldiers got high and were just lying back, saying, "I'm not going back out there!" He talked about some of the officers sending them out after a lot of soldiers were killed. Some of those officers were shot by their own men. But the army said they were killed in battle. Later on, it was all in the papers about this. They called it fragging.

I GOT TO BE A DIE SETTER after six months or so at the parts place. I would set up the dies for the machines to get going. I trained young people who came in, showed them how to run the press. If something was wrong, I found out what, maybe took the die out of the press, took it in to the skilled guys who worked on the dies. They fixed it, then I took it down and put it back in the press.

Once I started setting the dies, I asked the owner's son for a raise. The father was just like a regular worker, but the son had been to college and he was running the place for his father. "Well," he said, "the company isn't doing too good right now"—like I'm not supposed to know nothing, I am just a little worker.

I told him I had looked at those tags, what the order slips said General Motors was ordering, Chrysler, whatever. I told him, "You said the company isn't doing good. The company is doing damn good, the orders are way up there." I saw how many parts they ordered. "Look here," I told him, "I may not have all this education, you being an educated person, but I been to school on people like you. I know exactly where you coming from."

He looked at me, and then he said he would see could I get my raise.

But I didn't get my raise right away. I went to ask about it.

He said, "Don't worry about it, your raise will show up next check."

I got my check the next week. No raise on the check. So I went right into his office, just bust in the door.

He was in there talking to somebody, some sales person or somebody. He looked at me, "What are you coming in my office like that for?"

"This, this here is why I'm coming in." I held my check out for him to see.

He came on me like he was going to get rid of me, "You don't come in my office like that. If you don't like the job, you know what to do."

"Yeah I know what to do." We had got to that point.

I went on back out of his office. After he got done talking to the guy, he came out on my job, telling me I was wrong, but then he said he was wrong too, so we were both wrong. He took me outside the plant, and he told me he didn't want me to leave. So finally I got my raise.

Somebody says he'll do something, he is supposed to do it. That was what got me mad, why I went in his office like that.

MARTIN LUTHER KING was assassinated in April 1968. People were talking about it, mad. Some people came out in the streets. There was a little riot on the East Side. They brought cops in from all the suburbs, caravans of four and five cars riding together, going all through the city. They were coming in all through the area where I lived, four and five cars traveling together, patrolling. There was a curfew, you had to be off the street after dark. I guess they were afraid things would jump off again.

WE HAD A DEATH in the family, and I went down to Alabama with my brothers. We came back to Detroit late, didn't get back until four or five Monday morning, and we had to be to work at six. We were tired, drove the whole way. So we didn't go to work until the next day.

On Tuesday, the owner sent me home, gave me time off for not coming in. After he gave me the rest of the day off on Tuesday, I was fixing to walk around and get my car from my brother Willie. He worked about three blocks from where I worked. I was walking around there when he came in the car to meet me. They had given him a day off too.

Willie was mad. "You know what we ought to do, let's go out to Chrysler."

"OK."

So we went out to Chrysler. I got hired at Lynch Road, and my brother could have gotten hired too, but he didn't want to go onto the line. He had been off the line and he wanted to get into skilled trades. He had trained three years for that. So he didn't take that job. But about two weeks later, Willie was still pissed off, so he went out to General Motors. He got hired at Cadillac.

I started at $3.26 in August 1968, that's what assemblers were making back then. Janitors were making about fifteen or twenty cents less. They tried to put me to work the same day, on afternoons. But I couldn't start to work that night. So the next day at six a.m., I was there on the job.

IT WAS MY SECOND WEEK at Chrysler, and I got into an argument with the supervisor about the line speed. The job I had then, I connected some pieces in the back seat and then attached wires inside the trunk of the car with the line steady moving.

The foreman came up. I told him, "I done worked all kinds of jobs, hard jobs, and I never seen no shit fast like this before."

He said, "Well, that's the set-up."

"Well, what fool set this up then?"

It was the speed. You have just so many seconds to do a job. Then you get another car. If you don't do it fast enough, then you go into somebody else's area.

There was another guy doing a job in the trunk. He was getting behind on it, too. He was complaining to the supervisor about it. There was too much on the job to do it in that short a time. He was arguing with the supervisor, too, showing him how long it would take to do that.

That's why we got in the habit of messing with the supervisor. We'd done hard jobs before, but that speed was something else, and if something went wrong, you got behind. We had about four or five people. When someone had a problem, somebody else would call the supervisor over there, then by the time he would get there, somebody over here on a different job would call him. He'd be saying, "What?" We had it planned, time he get to one job, he would be called over to another job. We were messing with him.

AFTER I HAD BEEN THERE for a while, I got so I could do my job.

We would get off the line. We'd be acting so crazy, they thought we were fixing to riot again. Workers had the radio in the cars coming down the line turned up to the last notch, the music on. James Brown. The ones on this end hollering with him, "Say it loud, I'm black and I'm proud,

Say it loud, I'm black and I'm proud!" Someone on that end would answer back, "Say it loud, goddam it, I'm black and I'm proud!" Sometimes we would jump off the line to the side, be dancing. Those white supervisors, they'd just stand there looking like they didn't know what to do, what was going down. They acted like they were scared. It didn't take Chrysler long after that to get a lot of black supervisors.

We used to wrestle on the line. One of these guys—he was an ex-soldier—he couldn't get me down. He was surprised he couldn't get me down. His weight was around 230 pounds, height about 6-2 or 6-3. I was about 165 or 170.

Another was a young kid that just came in there, seventeen, not eighteen yet, but he got in there. Later they found out he wasn't eighteen, and they laid him off, but he got right back in there. He'd grab me, surprise me, run up on me so fast and lift me off the floor, but then I did a wrap move I learned from my uncle, my mother's brother. When I did that, whoop, he fell back on the floor and said, "How'd you do that?" I looped my leg around behind his—it was a snake wrap.

We were doing all this and it wasn't even on break time. We got to the point we could work ahead, then we'd start boxing, me and this young guy. He showed me all these moves he had.

I said, "I can do that, too, so let's do it then."

Some of those people were just wild and loose. They were just being themselves, right there on the job. They sure enough shocked the company.

BUT THE DRUGS were coming in. At that time, I didn't have any sense of what was going on. When the drugs came in, it helped destroy and break that unity people felt. Some of the most militant people got on drugs. Even if they were still working there, they were not going to act with the rest of the people. They'd be stealing from anybody, even from their parents or their kids. No unity. They'd just be thinking about how to get some money so they could get some drugs. I saw guys around there, some of them militant guys, some with groups on the East Side, some around people who called themselves Black Muslims—but they weren't the Muslims with Elijah Muhammad—they'd be sitting in there doing drugs. Those people that got hooked on drugs couldn't gather together no rebellion.

That went on about two or three years. The bosses let it go until the most militant people had got drug habits. The supervisors didn't say anything. The bosses probably told them, don't mess with them, long as they do their job, let them alone. And most of those guys did their job.

The heroin spread all over Detroit. Workers were doing drugs right beside the line. They'd sit on the side of the line at break time and do drugs like they were having lunch.

At break time, this guy Bob put the heroin on a little piece of cardboard. Instead of snorting on the side of the line, he went to the cafeteria with his little cardboard, supervisors and everybody out there. I don't know how he got there, but he left walking. That's what he was doing, had it on the cardboard and going to the cafeteria. That's how wide open it was.

There were a lot of drugs all over the place, a lot of heroin on the job and nobody was messing with you. In the street, cops looked the other way. They knew what was going on. But they didn't bust people. There were a whole lot of cops involved in what was going on with the drugs. Cops would come by one of the apartments where someone was selling drugs and tell them, "You better have some money for me or you're gonna have a problem." Some of those cops were selling. Some were just collecting money. It was open. They finally got rid of a bunch of those cops over at the Tenth Precinct on Livernois and Fullerton.

At the time I didn't understand it. Later I looked back

and saw what it really was. When I got more political, I knew. I could see exactly what happened. Before 1967, you could get pills and weed, but after '67, heroin got to be the big thing. They used to call it "the boy," which was a little stronger, and "the girl," different things like that. Then they mixed things, had a little cap of heroin with codeine or something mixed in it. But most people got away from that and just started snorting, just the heroin. Most dudes weren't shooting up, just snorting it.

It was enough. Those drugs coming in helped break the militancy.

IN 1968, I WAS LIVING with Ocie and Grace and their four kids on the corner of Woodrow Wilson and Seward. That's when I started using heroin. A girl I met from Chicago, living in a building nearby, was using and she got me on that stuff.

This guy from Alabama was robbing everybody, got everybody terrified. He was taking everyone's money— from the paper guy, the insurance guy, anyone so long as he could get some money and get away. He had a fight with someone and shot him three times. Everyone knew who he was. He was right there in the neighborhood.

He robbed me in the building right across the street from where I was living. We were in the drug house, and he came in just like anybody. He came in and pulled his gun, said, "Everybody on the floor." Then he went around taking from everybody's pocket.

I guess I didn't show fear when he robbed me because he struck me with his gun. "If you want to keep on driving that Bonneville, you'll keep your damn mouth shut and won't say nothing about it." That's the threat he told me, bumping me on the forehead with that big gun.

We all knew who he was, but he didn't care. One day, I was doing something in the trunk of my car, and he and another guy came by. He kept on walking, but the other guy stopped and said, "You want to buy a gun?" He told me what kind of gun it was. It might have been the gun that guy stuck me up with.

I told him, "No, man, I don't need one, I already have a gun." I know that Alabama guy heard me.

He also walked right up to my car later on. He saw a buddy of his on the passenger side, a guy who lived in the building. I no longer had the Bonneville; I had changed cars. If he knew it was me in the car, maybe he wouldn't have stopped, but he came over to talk to my rider. The minute he looked in the car and saw it was me, he cut his conversation, said, "Well, OK man, I'll talk to you later." He took off. He'd already stuck me up, he already heard me say I had a gun. I just may have a gun, he didn't know. So he took off.

A guy I knew was talking to me about it. He said the guy had robbed him, threatened him. I told him I had a problem with this sucker too. Since he was a bully, we were both thinking about stopping him. There were so many people that knew about him, his time was shortening anyway. Finally, he went to jail. He had shot and killed a guy down on Rosa Parks, and the cops finally tracked him down and picked him up. If he hadn't gone to prison, he probably would have been killed in the neighborhood.

AT THAT TIME, most of the white families had moved out of the neighborhood, just one or two left, like Squirt's family—him and his brother and their two sisters and their parents. They weren't ready to move out, they grew up there. His brother had a kid by one of the girls there in the neighborhood. If you would hear Squirt and his brother talking, you would think they were black. That's who they grew up with, and they talked the same way. If you didn't see them, you would definitely think they were black. They were young, just getting to be teenagers when the riot jumped off. They probably did a lot of looting through that area too.

WHEN I CAME to Michigan, it was mostly Jewish people who ran the little stores in Detroit. In the areas where I lived, Jewish people had been living all through that area. When they moved out, black people moved in. Some of the Jewish people sold the properties, some of them rented out the property for some time, then sold it. From Chicago to Grand Boulevard, and from LaSalle over to the Lodge Service Drive. There are some big houses over in there. Probably middle class people lived in those big houses before. But after the riots, mostly black workers took over the houses and some of the four-family flats. When the winter hit them, they couldn't hardly deal with the prices and pay the heating bill. They didn't have the money for it. The building was taking them down. Some of them turned around and rented rooms out to people they knew or somebody's friend to deal with the cost, or else they had to let the house go. They bought those big houses, but after they bought them, they couldn't afford them.

IN 1968, the Black Muslims were coming by the building, walking with their paper. In the summer, we'd be sitting on the porch, and they'd come up and I talked to them. They would come by pretty regular and we would talk. I got the paper from them. If I wasn't there, they'd leave it with my sister-in-law, then come back to talk, and I'd pay them. This Muslim guy I was talking to said I should come over to the Temple on Joy Road and talk to someone else.

In 1969, I had come to decide to join the Black Muslims. I was going to go over to the Temple. One of the brothers came by the house to take me over. But I had been hanging out the night before. I still had liquor on my breath. He told me, "You'll have to go another time. You won't be able to talk to nobody today. Why don't we go when you haven't been drinking."

133

So I guess I wasn't ready. I didn't ever go. If I hadn't been messing around with liquor and stuff, if I'd stopped then, I probably would have been in that organization. Those brothers from the Nation of Islam were the first people who showed me that they were ready to stand up for themselves. When you're just an individual, it's one thing. But there was an organization talking about fighting back against the problems.

I MOVED IN with my cousin Clarence Ware toward the end of 1969. Clarence was twelve years older than me.

Clarence was a person who didn't read at all. But he always worked—he just learned from what he saw people do. One time, I went back down to Bessemer from Detroit with Clarence driving. Even on the highways, he knew his way by looking at different landmarks. He knew where he had to turn to get off one highway onto another. Even from big trees, he knew where we were. He did that from Detroit—all the way through Ohio, Kentucky, Tennessee, before we got to Alabama—seven hundred and some miles. He kept that all in his mind.

Clarence got shot in the face one time by a guy whose wife was having a relationship with Clarence. The guy came and knocked on the door. Clarence came to the door, but the guy had gone over across the street, and he shot from across the street. Clarence was hit on the side of his face.

Clarence got his .22 rifle and came back down to his back door, and here come the wife, coming to tell Clarence her husband was on his way over. She didn't know he had already made it over there and shot Clarence. Clarence couldn't see well with blood running down his face. He just started shooting at the person who was running toward him. But it was her, the guy's wife. It was night and it was dark and she was running. When she started hollering, he knew. But he had shot her twice I think. He was using small bullets, a .22 rifle. Bullet went through her and came out the other side. Clarence called the emergency for both of them. They didn't press charges against Clarence.

Then Clarence moved. About a month after we moved, I was just coming in the door, getting ready to go to a party, and there was the guy that shot Clarence. I knew who he was because I had seen him at the other place, but he didn't know me.

He asked me, "Wonder if I could get in and go upstairs."

"I don't know about that, but if you tell me who you want to ring, maybe I can knock for you." I pulled the door closed real quick and locked it. Then I went up and told Clarence, "The guy's down there."

The guy took off when I told him I couldn't let him in. After an hour or so, I left and went to the party.

The guy came back. I don't know how he got in. Somebody let him in, or maybe he came in behind somebody. He was in the hallway, and he did the same thing again, knocked on Clarence's door. He must have found out which apartment my cousin lived in. He was already on probation, not supposed to come near the house, but he was back and shot again.

Clarence was lying down on the floor. His oldest brother had brought a shotgun over, told him, "Maybe you need a shotgun." He left it with Clarence. But Clarence was on the floor using his pistol. The guy ran out.

That guy did time because that was the second time he came around, shooting at Clarence. My cousin was at home both times. I had to go to court on that because I had seen the guy so I knew who he was. We were up there, and the judge got to looking back on this guy's record. He was not supposed to be near my cousin's house. Yet he came back there with a weapon again. They charged him with "attempted murder." They'd put him on probation for the first one, but for the second one, he had to do time.

I MOVED IN with another cousin in 1970, Betty and her husband Scarboro. They lived over near where I was hanging out. Clarence lived further away, maybe three miles away. I met Betty's husband when I came through Bessemer in 1967. He was hanging with me in Alabama, him and another guy, named Hunt. When I left, they were still in high school, the last year in high school. But they told me, "Man, I'm coming up that way, soon as I get out of school. I'm coming to Detroit." And they did, too.

But then Betty got sick and they moved back to Alabama. She had skin cancer from the job she was working. It was one of these chemical places. That's what she thought it was. Her skin was all messed up, and she started losing her hair. So she went back to Alabama. She didn't last that long. She died in 1971. She was only twenty-one or twenty-two.

I WAS REALLY addicted when I moved in there, and I started selling heroin to pay for it. Once you get addicted, you got to spend all your money to feed your addiction. I wasn't addicted more than some people, I wasn't running it, shooting it up. But still, you get a certain addiction, you are going to spend most of your money—that's where most of your money's going to go, especially if you are doing it every day. And I was doing it every day.

I just bought this small quantity—it was enough for four or five people, counting me. It was enough for me for two or three days, and then the guys around me at work got the rest of it. I would take their money, hold it until the heroin was gone, then buy another little bit for all of us. Two or three days later, run out, get another packet, get their money, turn it over again.

I was addicted. It's just like people can't go without smoking a cigarette. Same thing, but more so because it's stronger, you want to feel that feeling. You need it. Then, if you ain't feeling that feeling, you start to do more. And if you're at a party with people, you might do more.

They say crack is much worse. I knew people who were on heroin maybe for years, they kept working. But I never saw a guy so crazy like the ones on crack. I met this guy at the unemployment office, he said, "I had to let that shit go, the crack. It makes you so crazy, you have to rush right back and get more." I noticed people I'd been around, after just two years on crack, they were looking bad, very bad. Crack does something different to them.

I never used that crack. That came in later. But I used the heroin for a couple years, right up into 1971.

Eighteen
Chrysler's Dodge Main Plant

THEY SHUT LYNCH ROAD down in February of 1970. We were on a three-month layoff. They called us back in May, but instead of calling us back to Lynch Road, Chrysler transferred a lot of us over to Dodge Main, four hundred people, a whole line on the second shift. So we went over there and wound up working over there almost nine years until the plant closed in '79.

The first year, it wasn't too much different from other plants, working on the assembly line. It was about the same thing, just doing different operations. Plus when I got over to Dodge Main, since they knew I put windshields in at Lynch Road, they put me doing that.

We took the windshields and made sure they weren't cracked before we put them in. There were two of us putting them in. We put the glass in place, then we went around the edge of the glass with this little tool and pushed the glass inside the rubber to make it fit.

We were having a problem one time. The engineers had cut the design for the glass a little too big in one spot, and we were banging on it and banging on it, couldn't get the glass in. We were breaking the glass, trying to get it in. The supervisor wanted to get on us, talking about breaking the glass, like it was our problem. We kept telling him, "There's an engineering problem." The glass would hang up, it was cut too big to go in. We got some in. But we would get some that just didn't want to go in, whatever we did, they wouldn't go in. We were getting in the hole, trying to get glass in. And the repairman would get tied up because we were letting some of the glass go, and he was getting behind trying to get them in. That was a problem. I took one that was busted already from trying to get it in, picked it up and threw it out in the aisleway. Boom!

The supervisor saw me do it. When the glass hit the ground, he came running over, "What? What's wrong with you?"

"I told you, we got a problem here, this glass won't go in there. It was cracked anyway when I threw it out there."

They finally checked what we were talking about, and they found out that it was the engineering. The glass should have been cut a little bit smaller at one spot. But they didn't listen.

WE WEREN'T THERE very long when the GM strike started, September 1970. It was the end of the contract at Chrysler, too, right after midnight, September 15th. The Body Shop walked out. The Paint Shop went too, I think. And I had some people with me in Trim, about eight people. But some of the people were a little afraid. Supervisors were talking to them, trying to hold them back. We were walking out, and while we were walking down the line, we were telling other people, "We heading out of here. Why don't y'all come on, let's go."

When we got to the hallway to go downstairs, there came Labor Relations, and some of the workers started to turn back. The rest asked me, "What you gonna do?"

"I'm gonna join the party."

There were still two or three of them went downstairs with me, but then Labor Relations came down, threatening them. That's when the rest turned around and went back.

Body Shop and Paint were already out there, out on Joseph Campau raising hell. So I went out where they were. They blocked the road, and when cars came by, they yelled at the people, "Strike!"

The workers had a right when the contract expired to go out. That's what always used to happen. But the union didn't call Chrysler workers out in 1970, the leadership didn't call us out. The workers in the Body Shop went out anyway.

This guy Calvin who worked with me on the windshield had been looking out the window and saw people down there yelling, "If you're not out here by twelve, you better stay in there then." Something like that. "You better not come out this way if you don't come out by midnight." Some of them had got bottles and stuff, piled up those bottles.

When the other workers came out later, some of those Body Shop guys threw bottles and cans at them. There were a lot of them, the workers organized out in the street, and they were throwing things and the others were running, trying to get out of the way.

Calvin said, "The next time, I ain't gonna stay in here." And the next time we had a strike, Calvin was out of there. He wasn't going to stay in there again. So that was kind of funny.

CARS WERE JUMPING off the line. This was the last of 1970 or the first part of '71. Maybe something just fell in the track. Maybe someone put something in the track. I don't know how it first started. But every so often, one would come off at the bend of the line. Managers would be coming up, watching to see who did it. But they never could find out. A few hours later, maybe the next day, another car would come off. We'd get another break. One time Labor Relations and the top supervisors all came running up there. One of the cars had come off where the cars came up to the turn. Then the next car hit the first car that was off, ran up on that car in the back end of it, going up on that car. So another car was running off the track. That's when the foreman stopped the line. He said, "I ain't never seen no shit like this before!" They couldn't figure out why they were coming off. They couldn't figure that out at all.

Labor Relations and all of them were up there. But later on, after they left, another one came off. One of the workers, a Yugoslavian guy, went over there and hit the line button, stopped the line.

I talked to him and told him, "Hey, hold on, that's not your job to be stopping the line."

"Well the supervisor told me, if that problem came up, hit the button."

"Don't you want a break, an extra break? See what those other people are doing over there? You go over there, sit down, get an extra break, let the supervisor do it."

The company says that's sabotage. But most of the time when people do that, it's because they're working too fast on that line. They get a little extra time, get off the line for a minute. It's not that much. But it's something.

Sometimes, the line stops because the jobs are set up wrong. You complain, but they don't do anything about it. So you don't finish the job. Then someone coming after you can't do their job, then other people can't do their jobs. There's a repairman, he's got more time than you do. But when they keep coming, the repairman can't catch them all. So then a foreman has to stop the line.

People want that time. Once they stop the line, that's important, you get that break.

We'd get a break before lunch, and one afterwards, plus your lunch. Three times. But that's not much. That line was going steady all the time, fifty or sixty cars an hour, sometimes more. You had about a minute per car to get your job done, then the next one comes. And you had to get every one of them. If you had to go to the restroom and there was a "floater," an extra person, they'd put that person in, or they'd use the repairman for a few minutes. But it wasn't any time at all. If you got behind on your job, you were getting down in someone else's spot, throwing someone else off. They couldn't do their job. That's why, when the line stops, no one is mad. Why are you going to worry about it? Everyone gets an extra little break. "Break time!"

It happened all the time. A guy working up on the fourth floor before the cars came down was cutting the wires, taking the pliers and messing them all up. Then when the cars got down there to the inspection on the third floor, none of that stuff was working. They tried to find out what was happening, who was messing it up. They sent people up there watching me.

One of the guys—he was a guy who did different jobs, what they call a floater, going from job to job—he came down where I was. He told me, "Man, they talking down there. If you doing something, whatever it is, you better stop it, they looking."

I didn't even know what he was talking about. I didn't know what the problem was. But right after the floater came by, somebody from Labor Relations was standing across from me: two people, and one of the guys had a camera. I guess he was going to take a picture, thinking I was causing the problem. I wasn't working anywhere I could even do that. Finally they found out that it was coming from somewhere before me. They were watching me and the problem was still coming.

Afterwards I found out what happened. The guy who was doing it came to see me. People had told him that they were watching me, so he came down and told me that he was the one cutting that shit. He knew how it all went together, so he knew how to mess them up. He was pissed off. They had owed him some overtime money, and he had complained and complained, but they kept on not paying him, even knowing they owed it to him. He would come in expecting this big check, thinking his overtime would be on there, and it wasn't. So he was pissed off, that's why he was doing that.

Nineteen
Getting the Big Picture

NOT LONG AFTER I got to Dodge Main, I started reading this newsletter that was coming out, "Dodge Workers Speak." Then one day, I saw something that was written in it. I knew it was something I had talked about with this woman working in the next group from me, Judy, same department but different group. She used to work on down in my area, doing something with the trunk of the car, putting in the wire that runs for the light.

So anyway, here comes this thing I said right back at me. See, at lunchtime and break times we would be sitting around talking, a bunch of us. I had already checked her out, by listening to her, I knew she wasn't just an everyday person. When we were talking she could talk about so many different things. And the average worker didn't know about all that. She was the first person I ever met who talked about communism.

My mind was clicking now, figuring this out. So I figured out she was with this newsletter. Anyway it was something I had said, and it wound up in that paper. That was before they changed it to "Spark." I'm thinking maybe it was around 1971 they stopped doing the other one and started doing "Spark." But this was before "Spark" started when I read this stuff.

There was this other paper, "DRUM." Once in a while

they would pass out something. But not very often. Most of them were black nationalists. Some of them were real fighters. They had led some walkouts some years before. There were a couple decent guys still at Dodge. One of them had run for union office before I got there. But a lot of them were gone by the time I got there. The company fired a lot of them. And some, the company made supervisors. That was one of the things they talked about, getting black supervisors. So they got black supervisors, but they were still supervisors.

My supervisor worked with "DRUM" before he was a supervisor. We got into it sometimes. After all the things we'd been through, he came over one day and asked me, "Why don't you go down there and sign up for supervisor, they are hiring black supervisors." I think they had told him to do that because I was already a problem. They figured they would get rid of the problem if they got me to sign up for supervisor. But I just told him straight up, "Oh, so I can mess with people like you do? No, I don't want that supervisor job." I guess he went back and told them.

Maybe that's what Chrysler figured, they could get rid of the problem they had with militants by making some of them supervisors.

I started working with the "Dodge Workers Speak" newsletter, helping with it, but I wasn't passing anything out in the plant. A couple people were passing it out outside. But I used to give information. And I started to talk to different people working with that newsletter.

But at that time, I was still messing with the stuff, with the heroin.

CHRYSLER SUSPENDED ME in 1971. I got in a fight with Joe, a guy from my home town, too. He came straight from Gainesville up to Detroit. His daddy was close to my family. He lived, I think, next door to where my people were living. Joe was messing with Calvin, the young guy who worked with me, doing the windshield with me. Finally Calvin called him "black motherfucker." Calvin was real light skinned, and Joe took that to the point that Calvin was acting like he was white and prejudiced. But you know most of us do that, most blacks say things like that, but Joe took that different, like Calvin was acting white and disrespecting him.

So Joe kept threatening him that he was going to beat his ass. He kept coming up the line where we were.

I told Joe, "Man, why don't you leave that boy alone?"

That's how me and Joe got into it. He said he was going to kick my motherfuckin' ass, and I told him I would take him in that bathroom and turn that brain around in his head.

So he jumped off the line, and I went off the line behind him. Before we could get to the aisleway to cross to go into the bathroom, he grabbed this piece of board that had a nail sticking out of it. When he grabbed the board I tried to block it, and the nail cut my arm. I rushed him, knocked him on the floor, then I came out with my knife. I cut him a couple times, on the face, on the shoulder somewhere.

Big Will was near when it started, and he pulled me back off him and said, "Sam, Sam, stop, you're going to really hurt this boy. Stop."

They took me down to Labor Relations, and they took Joe down to Medical. They put us both out for the fight.

We were off not quite two weeks I think, suspended. Joe reported it to the police, filed charges. They were gonna pick me up, but Joe admitted he picked up this board before I cut him. After he said that, the police officer told him that was a weapon, too, and the other guy could file charges against him. And so he told them then, forget it. Edie Fox, the committeewoman, talked to the police, and that's what they told her. They didn't come get me, but we both lost almost two weeks for the fight.

Edie Fox got us back in there. She went in and talked to

the company. There wasn't any arrest, and I guess we were both good workers. But she was a very good representative. Much better than what you see today. She really stood up for the workers. And she was a militant fighter herself. She'd been around a long time.

So anyway, she got us back, but when they got us back, they put me on another floor. I worked down on the third floor, on different jobs, moving here and there.

BY READING the "Spark" newsletters and talking to people around it, I began to get a bigger picture of the U.S. system. I was reading things I hadn't ever seen before. You don't get that out of the system. That doesn't come out of the TV or the radio. I didn't get that in school. I got it from people working with the "Spark," and from the books I started to read. Before then, I didn't even know who Karl Marx was, or Lenin or Trotsky. I didn't know about Malcolm X or Robert Williams. I didn't know anything about the Russian Revolution. When you did hear something, you only heard the bad parts, didn't hear anything about what really happened, how workers took power, what happened after that. I began to see what the working class could do when it was brought together.

I began to get a bigger picture of the system. And I started paying attention to the news. Added to what I already understood from how I grew up, I began to see that as long as the capitalists control everything, it's going to keep getting worse for the majority of the people.

ONE DAY, we heard that this guy had burned to death in the paint oven. He was older, and he wasn't feeling good. Maybe he had high blood pressure, I forget. He had been to Medical, but he went back on the job. Somehow, he ended up inside the paint oven. I think it was after lunch when they started up the line, they found what was left of him. I don't know how hot those ovens got at that time, but they had to

147

be really hot to set the paint.

That man had a son working at Dodge Main when that happened.

Little Dave and I went all down the line talking about it. They had the technology to prevent that. They could have had an alarm on the line, to shut it down if someone got caught inside the oven. They could have protected workers' safety. They should have taken him out of there if he wasn't feeling good. We said, "They might as well have put a bullet in the man's head."

People were really upset. We went around with stickers and people put them up in the plant: "Chrysler Kills."

And we wrote about it in the newsletter.

Little Dave was from Alabama, a friend of my cousin Betty and her husband. He lived near me and worked at Dodge Main.

He knew I was talking to people in the Spark group. I tried to get him to talk to this young guy who passed out the newsletter at the gate. I was learning different things. I was trying to get other people interested. I thought Little Dave was someone who could get something out of these ideas.

I think they talked for a while. Afterwards, Little Dave said, "That guy, he's a nice guy, but he's not no fighter. How's he gonna tell me about people fighting." Little Dave had been in the streets. When people are in the streets, they read someone's attitude.

I sat Little Dave down, "Maybe he's not. But there's something he knows that you don't know, you can learn from him. He's not a fighter, but by you being a fighter, he can learn something from you. You can learn from each other." That made sense to him. He knew I knew some things he didn't know.

Little Dave died early. He was messing with stuff, different drugs. He tried to get off. He was taking that methadone. They said that stuff would help you get off. But people got addicted to that. That's what happened to Little Dave. That's how he died. It's a shame, because he was a fighter.

ABOUT THIS TIME, I stopped messing with drugs. I had started organizing. Judy fought with me about drugs for a while. She said to me, "If you're going to bring the brothers together, how are you going to do that, keeping them on the drugs? How in hell are you going to bring the brothers together when you mess their minds up?" She'd argue with me, "You're messing your own mind up. You're letting the man get over on you." She kept after me, "Everybody knows what you've been doing. Maybe the people who are into that don't care. But the people who are not into that, what do they think? You're trying to tell them something, why are they going to listen to you? Why should they trust you?"

That's when I started thinking about that, and what the drugs were. I pulled back. I had to let the drugs go. I really wanted to bring the brothers together. When you do the drugs, it slows you down. You know it. When you see guys hooked on the stuff, they're addicted. You get high, you don't care. When I understood what I was doing, I understood there was something I needed to do. I had to let that go. I stopped using, and I stopped getting it for other people.

I STARTED SEEING other things. I used to be a gambler. You're trying to get workers to stand together. If you feel that way, if you want to take them forward, you can't take their money. You definitely can't do that. I've got my little bit of money and I'm going to take theirs too—that's definitely going in the wrong direction. I'm trying to get people to get together to help themselves. How could I take the little bit they got?

I NEVER WENT to a union meeting until I went to Dodge

149

Main. There wasn't any union at most of the other jobs I had. There was a union at Lynch Road, but I don't remember ever going to a meeting. Maybe I talked to a steward. When I started working at Chrysler in 1968, I didn't see myself being active in the union. Maybe I was too busy doing my own things, messing with drugs, drinking and running in the streets. But I just figured the union was supposed to be dealing with the problems, and whoever was in office, that was their job. The committeemen and stewards, they are the union—that's what I thought. And most of them wanted the workers thinking that they'll take care of it, the workers don't need to do anything. It's got worse today, but even then, most of them didn't try to get people involved.

I was like a lot of workers today, I didn't see that the union isn't anything unless it means all of us. I didn't see that the union means if they're messing with you, then they're messing with me. You don't see that until you get into a fight against the company, and see what you can do when you stand together. I didn't start going to union meetings until I started to learn certain things in history about the power of the working class.

WE WERE ALL talking about this guy George Jackson in the summer of 1971. Guards killed him in prison out in California and then a riot jumped off in Attica prison in New York, protesting his murder. They said George Jackson was trying to escape. We didn't believe it. There was all that security at San Quentin, and he was unarmed—he couldn't get out, no way. No, they wanted to kill him, was what it was. He was writing about what was happening in the prisons. What he wrote was going to other prisons, so he was well known. I read something by him at that time.

THAT SAME YEAR, I went up to Black Lake. Edie Fox got me and a couple other workers on the list to go up there.

She was the committeewoman for the Trim Department who got me back when I was fired. The reps could get people to go to Black Lake, but they usually put the same names down, the reps and other union officials. But Edie tried to get new people to go. That's how I got there.

Black Lake was a kind of vacation place the UAW had. The union got us off work and paid for us, paid our wages when we were off work. We went up there on a bus on Friday, and came back on Sunday. It had a big swimming pool, places to walk. Later on, they built a golf course. It was just like a resort. It was a place the bureaucrats could show off when they brought people there. I guess it was supposed to make you feel the union was important and you were part of something, to make you fit into the bureaucracy, try to make you think like them.

Black Lake is mostly for the people on top. They act just like the top people at the company, trying to make you feel how important they are. They bring people in there to make you think like them. They had classes about the union, but they didn't talk about workers' fights.

The people who came there, a lot of them fell into the bureaucracy, forgot about the workers' fights. Some of them never knew about the fights. They brought them in, trained them on the way they do it. But that's not what the workers need.

At that time, I couldn't see all that. I could just see that there were some top union people there, acting just like the bosses.

Twenty
Organizing Workers, Elected Steward

JOHN CAME INTO Dodge Main in 1973. He was curious about the "Spark." Who was this old guy out there on Jos Campau, passing out the newsletter, working with the "Spark"? John was a young guy when he came in there.

He talked to the guy out front, but he wanted to find out who was working with the "Spark" inside the plant. He finally ran up on me, and we began to talk. John wanted to get involved. So he began to work with us, too.

We began to organize a lot of people around us. We had a whole crowd of different nationalities. I had black workers around me, and a few whites, and there were some Yugoslavian and Albanian, and Arab workers from different places like Palestine and Yemen. I knew a lot of guys from all those places. We had a couple guys with us that translated the "Spark" newsletter, a couple of Arab guys and one Yugoslavian and one Albanian. A couple different times we had three different languages in the newsletter. So that was something too, it got us known as a group. Some of the Dodge Main workers had not been here that long and didn't read much English, so that's why we did it. They could speak, but reading, they couldn't read English that well.

We also put out stuff about the union and translated that. John had two guys working near him who could translate, and there was another guy they knew that used to translate for us too. He was a teacher and he had been in different political fights back in his home country.

So we had all these people working with us. At the gate, sometimes we had seven people passing out union flyers at the gate, so we could talk to other workers coming in.

We had started a little class, a class about workers' fights and communism and the history of workers' struggles, just a few blocks from the plant, I forget exactly where it was now. We would stop there before we went into work, then just leave there and go on in. That's how we got a chance to organize some of those workers too. We had some different people to come. A lot of times they didn't come every time. But we were steady trying to get other people to come and be involved. I gave classes, too, talking to those workers about things I had read about, what workers had done in this country or other countries, things the workers had done, things those workers never heard about before. We wanted workers to know about these things. I never did something like that before. But I did that.

Then we would have meetings at lunchtime when the lines shut down. We would have meetings right there sitting up on top of the cars or in the break areas. There'd be problems, and we talked about what we could do. So we really had a lot of activity going on.

Workers around us began to school the supervisors. We had one supervisor, a little guy, he used to be wanting to show he was tough. One day at lunch when everybody was gone but the tools and things were still there, someone took some air guns and threw them someplace. When all the workers came back, the line started up, and their guns weren't there. The little supervisor was running around there like crazy, asking who did it.

No one knew anything! "When I left on break they was there, when I came back, they was gone." That's what they all said.

He ran and got some old stuff, but that wasn't enough. In that supervisor's area, four or five workers couldn't work because he couldn't get enough air guns. So they had to stop the whole line because too many cars were going down without the work done and no repairs. He quieted down some then.

Other supervisors learned it didn't pay to mess with us. I told some workers what we'd done at Lynch Road with a supervisor who caused us problems. If he was messing with someone, someone else would call him to the other end, yelling, "I got a problem here." Then someone else had a problem. We'd send him a message. So workers around us started doing that.

You think you can do something to mess with us, and we can't do anything to mess with you? Wrong.

THE MACK STRIKE got to be an issue at Dodge Main. That was August 1973. There were safety problems at Mack. It was a stamping plant. A couple people lost their hands in presses. The presses had problems and workers had brought that up, but management didn't deal with it. They just wanted to keep those presses running. So people got injured. And a guy was killed when a press came down on his head. Workers at Mack had done a few protests there already. I was down to Mack when the strike was going on. A man showed me his hand, how he had part of his hand cut off in a press.

I don't know exactly everything that happened. There was some kind of sit-down. Some Mack workers around a group called Progressive Labor did something that started that. But hundreds of workers stayed in the plant for a couple days. That's when the cops came in and tossed everyone out.

The strikers had a meeting to organize picket lines at all the gates for the next day. Maybe five hundred people were at that meeting.

The UAW tried to say it was "outsiders" who kept the

workers out, and the workers had no business in that strike because outsiders were involved. UAW officials came up to Mack the next morning with sticks and bats and other things. A thousand of them, Local union officials, Regional and International staff. Those goons chased the workers' picket lines away from the gates, then threatened everyone else, telling them, "If you don't go in, you'll be fired." They acted like the company, not a union.

I was working afternoons, so I went out there that morning to support the picket lines. But before I got there, I ran into John. He said, "They're running people away from there with bats and sticks and bricks." When John came running, a little kid there saw what was happening and told him, "Hey man, you can hide behind the house." He was little, but he already knew!

When I went back to work, I started to talk to people about what happened. I said, "We're not going to have that at Dodge Main. Don't let those gangsters think they can come here." And I said it loud, so the steward could hear it.

Joe Davis came down to my job. Somebody had told him I was talking about stuff at Mack. He was a committeeman then, but he was getting ready to run for president of the Local. Joe had been at Mack in the goon squad, doing the company's dirty work. He was over there, but I guess he didn't want anyone at Dodge Main to know about it.

He told me, "If you know what's good for you, you'll keep that Mack shit out of your mouth."

I came right back at him, "If you're making that a threat, if you're thinking about having your boys jump me, they better do a good job. If they don't, I'll be coming looking for you!" And I told him I wasn't only going to talk about it, we were going to put out a flyer about it. I got loud and Davis walked off. He was trying to keep it all just a private thing between him and me.

The workers were asking me, "What's all that about?"

So I told them: "Instead of fighting for the workers, those goons were fighting against the workers. They were doing the company's dirty work. We don't need a company union." We put out a leaflet, John and me, talking about what we saw at Mack. In the leaflet we said, "They said that only outside agitators were involved. That's a lie! Why were over 100 workers fired? They said that Mack workers were tricked and forced to go on strike. That's a lie too! The workers knew that Chrysler caused the problem and they had to fight back." And we told the workers, "Many people who organized the UAW were called outside agitators."

The "Spark" newsletter came out that next week, talking about those union reps that went over to Mack, who went out and did the company's job, breaking the workers' strike. It said, "Let them try that here. It's ten thousand of us here. We can show them they can't get away with that here."

Davis thought I was writing the "Spark," I guess because certain words and things I would say came out in the newsletter.

I WAS GOING to the Labor School at Wayne State University from the fall of 1972 to the spring of 1974 to get more training. I went to school during the day, working afternoons, a couple times a week. I was already thinking about running for steward, and I wasn't just jumping up for the steward's job, without knowing how the union did things.

One day at the Labor School, one of these skilled trades guys was there, talking: "The doggone production workers, they think they should be making more money than we make. They complain and act up, but they want to make more than the skilled trades do. I had to buy tools and other things."

When someone talked like that, I had to say something: "Hey, man, look here. Look. Those production workers that you are talking about—we don't hardly have time to get off the line and get a drink of water, and you are going to tell us what we don't need to be making? OK, skilled workers have training, and they have to pay for their tools, so they should be paid for that. But look at the time you have. Look at our job, look at what we're doing. Hell, look at all the work we do, and don't have time to get a drink of water. If we do, we get harassed and wrote up because we miss a job. That's how bad it is, if you get a drink of water, your job is going down the line. Conditions like that, we should be paid as much as anyone else."

He shut up after I started preaching.

That's how the skilled trades were sometimes, thinking they were better than other workers. It's not just skilled trades. Some people come to be a supervisor or get a slightly better job, they think they're better than the rest of us. It's not just the whites that think that way. I've seen that in a lot of black people I know. That's pushed on us—dividing the class, making workers fit into the system and start to think the way it works for the bosses. This capitalist system does that. It makes someone think he's better than the rest of us because he's skilled trades or because he's a supervisor. I'm not saying we're better than them, but we're as good as they are.

GOING TO THE LABOR SCHOOL gave me a chance to go to Washington, D.C. for a demonstration against the Viet Nam war in the fall of 1973. I went down on the bus with some of the students from Wayne State. We had a couple of buses. There was a Chinese guy on the bus, and a young white guy made some kind of racist statement against him. The young Chinese guy told him, "You don't even need to be going if you are making that kind of statement." He was right. We were going down there to stand against that war. Anyway, that white boy shut up then.

We got to Washington, but it took overnight to get there. We got there early in the morning before daybreak. Later on that day, I met some people from Baltimore who were selling the "Spark" paper down there. I knew them a little bit, so I talked and went around with them. We were just down there that one day and then that night we left back out. I remember there being about seventy thousand people or so down there. I got a chance to meet and talk to some of the Wayne students on the bus. I think they knew I was an auto worker. And I talked to a teacher from Wayne on the bus. She had just started teaching. I thought she was a student, but she was just a new teacher.

I went to protests and demonstrations after that, but that was my first demonstration in Washington. And it was the last big demonstration against that war.

Sam, 1974 election, Dodge Main

IT MAY HAVE BEEN the next year, 1974, when I ran for steward. I ran for steward, and John ran for my alternate. It was a big district, over two hundred people in it.

We talked about what the union should do, like having meetings in the plant regularly so workers could be there. We made a big point that we would defend every worker. No trading off grievances, no favoritism. We said we would let people know what was happening, give out information when we got it. And we said the membership should control the union, decide what we were going to do. We kept telling people we weren't going to promise to take care of things for them, that no one can do that—it will take all of us working together to change things.

On lunch time when the line was down, we would go around together, talking. We'd give workers one of our leaflets, and they'd know who we were from talking to us. We asked them to give the leaflets to other people. Our main leaflet was called, "A Workers' Program for Steward Elections."

People knew we were saying something different from what the others were saying. And I think it made sense to them. They'd seen people run for office before, run a con, then do nothing when they got in office. But we were talking something different.

At some point, I put out a leaflet called "Black Workers Can Lead the Fight." I said that black workers had a better understanding of the system and what it takes to fight it because of what we'd been through. But I also said that some people had thought if we got black foremen that would solve our problems, but we got them and it didn't change anything because they were still bosses. We got black union leaders and it didn't change, mostly because they had the same policy as the old white union leaders, going along with the company. And I said I would use my understanding as a black man to fight against the company and deal with the problems of all the workers. I said that all of us are oppressed as workers, and it would take all of us to fight, but black workers have experience and can lead the fight.

159

A WORKERS' PROGRAM for STEWARD ELECTIONS

1. All workers should unite in our own defense, because we are the ones being attacked. When the company attacks one of us it is an attack on us all. A steward should never say, "Don't worry about it. I'll take care of it." Because he can't. It will take us <u>all</u> working together.

2. The membership should control our union at all times. The members should make all the decisions. The union leadership's job is to carry out those decisions. I believe that when we put an end to all the secret bargaining, secret agreements, and secret deals, that we will have a much stronger union. The grievance procedure needs changing. Now, a worker is guilty until proven innocent. This should be reversed.

3. I would fight the continuous attacks of the company. For example:
   a) fight against the harassment and discrimination of all workers
   b) fight all racism against black workers, Arabian workers and other foreign workers
   c) fight against the harassing of workers for absences
   d) fight against all speed-up
   e) fight against the refusal to deal with safety problems

4. I promise to defend every worker. I would not play favoritism because only the man gains from this. I would file grievances, follow them through, and report them to all the workers. I promise that no worker's grievance will be traded off against another worker's grievance. I would keep all workers informed by posting information and grievances. I would help to organize support for any worker the company attacks.

5. I would call for regular meetings in the district as well as in the department. I would help workers all over the plant get together. We should have a line steward for every foreman.

I am running for steward in trim unit, 2nd shift, 3rd floor and 4th floor.

SIGNED: Sam Johnson, group 23,
3rd floor, trim,
2nd shift.

. . .

Anyone agreeing with this program and interested in making it happen, should talk to me or others supporting this campaign.

labor donated

Leaflet Dodge Main: A Workers Program for Steward Elections

BLACK WORKERS CAN LEAD THE FIGHT

I am a black worker in the Trim Department. I am running for steward for second shift on the third floor and part of the fourth floor

I believe that black workers can lead the fight for all workers. Black people in this country have been the victims of discrimination and harassment all of our lives. We have suffered under this society more than other peoples. We have been forced to fight back just to survive. So black workers have a better understanding of what this system is all about and how to change it.

BLACK LIKE US, BUT A BOSS LIKE THE OTHERS

In the past, some black workers thought if they had more black foremen and blacks in high positions, that it would solve the problems of racism. And then things would be better for black workers. Now we have black foremen and blacks in those high positions. But the problems still remain. Those blacks have to carry out the same policies for the bosses that the white foremen did.

Having black foremen and blacks in high positions is not the solution.

BLACK LIKE US, BUT RUNS THE SAME GAME AS THE OTHERS

Black workers tried to get more black representation in the union. They thought they would get better representation from blacks. We saw this take place in our local. The leadership changed from white to black. Black workers were looking for black leadership, but some con men used this feeling to get ahead for themselves. We saw this happen in the last election where so-called black militants lined up with a white racist who kept black workers out of skilled trades for years. Those representatives carry out the same policy that the old white leadership did. They are on the side of the bosses, and not on the side of the workers. The present leadership -- both black and white -- use the union to keep the workers from fighting back against the bosses. We do need black leaders, but of a different kind.

I will use my understanding as a black man to fight against the company and deal with the problems of all the workers.

BLACK WORKERS CAN LEAD THE FIGHT

There are many people who are oppressed in this country. Arab workers today face much of the same racist harassment. And white workers, Chicanos, Puerto Ricans, native Indians and other nationalities all have rotten conditions. It will take the organizing of all the workers in order to deal with the fight against the bosses.

I believe that black workers can lead the fight. We have shown that we will fight against racism and against the bosses' policies. We can begin to organize all the workers to change the conditions.

I am running for steward in this election to begin organizing workers now. And also to give workers who agree with these ideas a chance to show their beliefs.

                    SIGNED: SAM JOHNSON, Group 23, 3rd floor,
                                           2nd shift, Trim
                                           For Steward

(labor donated)

Leaflet Dodge Main: Black Workers Can Lead the Fight

We began to get a lot of support, and people were taking our leaflets around for us.

We challenged the steward and alternate to debate at lunchtime, one debate on the third floor, one on the fourth. We told people to come to the debate. People came up there, about thirty-five to forty people to both of them.

The debate was supposed to be between us and the stewards, but Joe Davis showed up to the first one. He was going to come, try and take over the debate. He had other reps and stewards with him too. When workers would try to say something, those reps would talk them down. Instead of letting the steward state his position, Joe Davis did most of the talking for him. Davis raised something about Mack, but he made it like the strike was all some outsiders, some political group that shut that plant down. If people voted for John and me, the same thing would happen at Dodge Main. He was talking about a friend of mine, saying my friend was out there and shut the Mack plant down. A guy I knew, by the name of Clarence, jumped up on the table and yelled, "What? She shut it down? You gotta bring her over here then!" Workers laughed and clapped.

Then Davis raised this other issue, "You don't want to put this guy in office, because if he gets mad with you, he'll go around cutting your throat." They all went around saying that. I said, "Anybody wants to know about this incident he is talking about, ask the people in that area what happened." And I left it like that.

They also went around saying, "Sam isn't writing any of those things, he's got that white boy writing up those leaflets. That white boy, he'll be running things."

I told people, "I'm the one running for steward, John's going to work with me. People who are busy have secretaries to help them out. What's wrong with that? Anyways, let's look at it from the workers' point of view. We all have to stand together as one. That's what makes us stronger. Stand together, not just for blacks, not just for Arabs, not just for whites, stand together for all of us. That's what it means, unity, stand together."

They did a lot of dirty campaigning—that went on all the time at Dodge Main. Davis and others running the Local thought they had it under control, and that we wouldn't win. But we beat them out and got in. Actually we did, we got elected.

THE DISTRICT was spread out on three floors of that old plant, third floor, fourth floor and a handful on the second floor, all in the Trim Department. I was the steward, but when I missed days, John would be on the floor. We worked it out that way, and it worked out pretty good.

There were little break areas with tables off the line. That's where we'd campaigned. So we started having meetings in those areas at lunch time. We'd tell people in one area that we were going to meet there at lunch time, "Tonight, we're going to have a lunch time meeting." People came. Mostly it was people from that area who came. Sometimes from different floors, but they were all from our district. People seemed to like it.

Mostly we'd talk about the problems workers had. If it was a problem that was a contract violation, we would write those problems up right there.

We had a totally different thing happening in our district than what was happening before. Workers had problems, but they didn't have a way to raise them together. Local meetings were only once a month. We said, "You don't have to wait for a membership meeting. If you have a problem, we can talk about it now, at lunch time."

I know the company didn't like it, and those meetings were a problem for the union bureaucracy, too. People were telling them, "Sam and John are having those meetings, why y'all ain't doing it?"

People would complain about a supervisor. We'd leave the meeting, go talk to him, ask him, "Why you messing with people? Why not let them do their jobs?" We'd front him off with workers standing around.

After we were elected, we discussed with people that they should have their own line steward to keep track of the problems, get people together to handle them if they could. One line steward for each foreman. "When the steward's not around," we said, "you can talk to the line steward, give him that information. It's not just the top, the workers themselves can run things. We're all involved in this here. That's what makes a strong union." We met with each group and told them, "You decide who would be the best person." And they did that. We elected those line stewards in the meetings. We had a line steward in just about every area. In some of those areas, we had two, in case one of them was off work.

They started keeping track of things the foremen were doing. They didn't have to wait for the steward to come. They collected all the information themselves for what needed to be done.

That shocked the foremen. They'd do something, and the same day, they'd have a grievance coming at them. The line steward gave me what they wrote up, I would talk to John, and he'd write that grievance on his break. I'd take it in that same day that something happened. And workers would see that.

We put out leaflets to everyone in the district, telling them what all their rights were.

If nobody in the union said anything different, supervisors would say, "We don't have no gloves now, we'll get you some tomorrow." So people would think they had to work like that. The foreman would tell them they had to do someone else's job, or get their own stock, or fix their own tools. He'd tell them to go out of their areas to catch jobs, or wait until break time to go to the toilet or medical. He'd put them on a job that violated their medical restrictions. And people wouldn't know. We were trying to let people know these things, what they had to do, and what they didn't have to do.

Someone would ask a question, so we knew a lot of other people would have these same questions. Like with SUB pay or overtime. Someone would ask a question, we would put something out about it. Workers could have something in their hands, information about what the rules are. Not like the usual union language that no one can understand, put out in small print, so no one understands what it means. That's what the union does, just like the company. We made it understandable and readable. And we put things on the board workers could find to check up on questions they had.

Getting that information out made people more ready to stand up for themselves.

Some of the union officials were speaking out against our lunch time meetings. One of the union committeemen stopped us, told us, "You can't be having meetings on company property. That's a big problem."

"What do you mean? You're telling us we can't talk at lunch time? It's our lunch time. Yes, we can talk."

AT ONE OF THOSE lunch time meetings, we found out that some workers had problems with their paychecks. Chrysler owed people all this back money. They had worked overtime hours, and the company owed them for those hours, but it just went along not paying them. Some of those people had been owed for as long as a year, and they'd never got their money.

So we said, "Come on, let's go down to the superintendent's office and talk about this money. We'll go down and have lunch with the superintendent." We didn't walk off the job, it was lunch time. "We'll have lunch down there today."

I told some of the people when we were getting ready to

165

go down there, "I don't care if it was five years ago, if they owed it, they owed it. They owe you, and they should pay you."

So we got down there. We had about twenty-five or thirty people come down there. Not all of them were owed money. But they wanted to know, "What's going to happen when y'all go down there?" They were up there for those other workers, going to see what the company was going to do. When all those people got up there, they were a force. Their numbers sent a bigger message to the company than a steward ever could. The workers saw that, because they had their money the next day. They saw what happened when workers stand together.

I talked to a few of them before we got in there. "Now, when you get in there, let that superintendent know how you feel about your money they owe you." I told them, "Let him know."

The workers thought they were going to stand outside, and John and me would go inside. But I said, "Uhn-uh! Come on in, here's the man you want to talk to."

The superintendent's office was full. And some of those workers were loud. That superintendent was scared. He didn't know we were coming down, we didn't tell him. And there were all those workers. He didn't know what they were going to do.

When we got in there, this guy named Pasmo got around behind the superintendent. He was right there behind him, and he got loud, "I'm getting tired of this shit, they been owing me for this money, and they know they owe me, and they still ain't paid me. I want my money."

The superintendent called Labor Relations and said, "There's all these people here." They must have told him, "Get the steward," because we heard him say, "Well, he's down here with them!"

So then he called Joe Davis to come settle the workers

down. Joe was a committeeman then, but he was campaigning for Local president. He had to come all the way from the other side of the plant.

He got there, out of breath, and he said, "What's going on, man?" He told me, "Come on outside the office, I want to talk to you."

One of the workers said, "What you got to say? You can say it right here." That's what one of the workers told him.

So Joe Davis told those people, "You know we got procedures to go by."

I said, "We done been through that, and they still haven't given these people their money. That's why they're down here. We done went through your procedures, so let's see what these people can do."

Then Joe Davis told us, "You have to come out of here."

And I said, "Let me tell you something, either you with us or you with them. If you with us, then come on and stop backpedaling then."

Finally, the superintendent told the workers, "We're going to deal with it. You'll get your money."

OK, so we said, "We'll wait and see."

Then we were out of there. We all went back together to where they worked. They talked to the people they worked with, told them what happened up there. Everyone was talking about it.

The next day, people came in, and they got their checks. But the company gave the checks to Joe Davis for four or five of these people. He went around and said, "See, you didn't have to go through all that; you didn't have to go down to the office, I went up there and got y'all's checks."

The workers just looked at him. They saw the game. One of the Arab workers came straight out and said to him, "Why give checks to you? You do nothing. They should have give the checks to Sam, the steward. You do nothing."

But that's what the company did, gave the checks to the

committeeman to make it seem like the workers didn't have to do anything. But why did they get their checks then, after all that time? Because of what they did.

So that was that, and a lot of people saw that, saw that when you bring together a lot of workers and make a force, it makes a difference. The very next day they had the checks. Not everybody because, with some of them, the old steward didn't write a grievance about the missing money, so we had to write the grievance first before they got them. But the others, they had their checks the next day.

So we did other things like that in those first months.

WE ALSO PUT OUT leaflets to the plant about issues that came up, giving workers information.

One of those issues was how often to have Local elections. In the Steward Council, they wanted me to sign a statement in favor of elections every three years, instead of every two years, the way it had been. They said it would save the Local money if we didn't have to pay for elections so often.

But I didn't look at it that way. I told them, "With three years, if the workers want someone else, they have to wait. Why should the workers have to wait three years if a steward isn't doing his job?" I told them I wouldn't sign that.

With three years, once a lot of these people got in there, they had more time to run their games. Most of what they were worried about was to have more time to do what they wanted before they got voted out. They wanted more time to use the Local's money the way they wanted. Two years, that's enough, more than enough.

It wasn't a surprise that they pushed that through the Local meeting, all the people the bureaucrats can bring to a meeting. All those people who had a position and wanted to keep it, all the people they gave little privileges to, all those people they got off the line for "union" time. All the people they sent to different conventions and conferences. All those people they were training to be like them.

ANOTHER ISSUE we brought up was the wildcat strike at Chrysler's Dodge Truck up in Warren. In the Steward Council, Davis talked about putting together a goon squad at Dodge Main in case there was any strike there. He didn't call it "goon squad," but that's what he meant. They were trying to say it was outsiders up at Truck that caused that wildcat. No, Truck workers came out of there when the company fired a steward they liked. It was Truck workers on the picket lines. And the bureaucrats up there attacked them.

We got all the line stewards and other workers in our district to sign a leaflet. We put it out at the gate to the whole plant, a bunch of us standing in front at the gate. Workers who were coming in stopped, helped pass it out, and some of them called the union officials gangsters.

We said to the workers, "If the goon squad comes here, we can deal with them. We're 10,000 strong." After what they'd done at Mack and Dodge Truck, we said that's what they were getting ready to do against workers at Dodge Main.

WE ORGANIZED a picnic for our district in August of 1974 at Elizabeth Howell Park. We had a lunch time meeting a couple weeks ahead for anyone ready to work on it. We called on people to come to a picnic with their families and friends. We asked people for $1 for each person and 50¢ for children under ten. We used it to buy hamburgers, hot dogs and drinks, and we asked people to bring their own dishes. We played some softball and volleyball, and we had checkers and chess contests. Some of the Arab workers were real good at playing soccer. So they were teaching some of us how to play. And we taught them how to play a little softball because they weren't up on that. I can't find anything on how many people came, but I know it was a pretty good little crowd.

IN 1974, the oil companies pushed gas prices up, and there was talk about the Arabs doing it. There was some talk in the plant against Arab workers, some people trying to say the Arab workers in this country were part of the problem. So the Arab workers had a protest demonstration around Woodward in the downtown area. John and I went down with some of the Arab workers from Dodge Main we were close to. The Arab workers at Dodge were trying to say, "You think we can't fight, eh?" Well, there was enough of them walked out of the plant, the plant had to shut down. Chrysler couldn't get production out that day.

SEPTEMBER 1974, the company and the union snatched us out of office. We'd only been in office six months. Chrysler laid off workers, and after that layoff, the company said the union had to cut back on stewards because they didn't need all that representation for the number of workers left in there.

At first, they were talking about cutting three reps. But the union leaders said they negotiated with the company, and the company agreed to cut only one. That was supposed to be a big victory, cutting only one. But who was that steward the company and union officials agreed to cut? That was me.

In the past, when they had to cut a steward, they would pick the smallest district to eliminate, with a hundred people or less. I had a large district, two hundred and some people. But I had to go!

Some of the workers were saying, "Why in the hell they chose you, and you are the best steward in here?" Some of the Polish guys talked to me. Some of those guys had been very prejudiced, especially the older ones. But one of those guys stopped me and said, "How in the world—what's wrong with this union? You are the best steward that I've seen in this doggone place. And they are going to cut you? Remove you?" I said, "Yep, that's what they said."

I told the workers, "We were not only pushing the

company, but we were pushing the union, and that was a problem for them too. We were doing things they were not ready to do. That's why the union went right along with the company to get rid of us."

WE FOUGHT THAT for a long time. Fifty-five workers from our district went to the big Local union meeting to support us. We talked to the workers ahead of time and told them, "When we stand up in the meeting, you stand up with us." And they did that. The bureaucrats started looking then.

But the bureaucrats can always turn out people when they want to vote you down. We lost the vote by just over a hundred to a little more than seventy. Even so, the Local president said he didn't want any workers thinking that they had the right to decide on which steward would be removed!

After the vote, we put in a protest, then an appeal to the UAW president's office, then appeal to the International Executive Board, and they sent us to a hearing at the Region, then back to the International Executive Board. At every step, we were turned down, one after the other. Then we went to the union's Public Review Board, and the International Executive Board reversed itself and decided we did have the basis for an appeal. Finally, sixteen months later, in January 1976, the International Executive Board ordered the Local to reinstate us or to schedule a new election and allow me to run in it.

Nothing happened, so finally I went to see the Local president, Joe Davis. He said he couldn't put me back because the company refused to let me be the steward!

"What? The company didn't put me in as steward. The workers did, they voted for me. So what does the company have to do with who the steward is?"

But that's what the union was like, carrying out what the company wanted.

Anyway, he told me the Local would run a new election

for steward. We went to the Local meeting, and we were told we had to take it up in the Trim Department meeting if we wanted an election—and then they cancelled Trim meetings for three months!

That went on for almost two years, almost up to the point it was time for new elections.

That's why workers get fed up, why they don't go to union meetings. It doesn't matter what the rank-and-file workers decide. Unless the workers are really organized, the bureaucracy just runs right over them. The bureaucracy was rotten then. And it's gotten a lot worse today. When there aren't enough workers standing up fighting, they can do whatever they want.

Twenty-One
Continuing to Organize—Without a Union Title

STARTING IN THE FALL of 1974, I was back to work on the line. They put me up on the fifth floor, not in my old district. I didn't have a regular job, they were moving me around. But I still was organizing and doing different things. John was laid off, but there were other people working with me, a couple guys, both named Clarence, and some others, six or seven of us in a little group, working together.

We started having lunch time meetings on the fifth floor. We tried to do that wherever there were people who wanted to get together. The Local union meeting was on a Sunday. A lot of times, given people's lives, they were doing other things, they had other plans for that day off, they didn't show up. With a lunch time meeting, they were right there together, so more workers came.

AT ONE LUNCH TIME meeting, someone suggested we do a picnic like the one we did when I was a steward. So we called for a lunch time meeting for anyone willing to work to put the picnic together.

When workers get together, you can find someone to do just about anything that needs to be done. Some workers knew about places to get the meat and other food, or charcoal and everything else we needed. When people get involved in something, they want to make it nice, do a good job setting it up. That's what makes a difference. And workers understood that, those workers did who came to those meetings.

We sold tickets in the plant and standing in front of the plant gates. And we told people we needed to know who was coming so we could know how much food to buy. We collected $2.50 for adults, $1.25 for children eight to fifteen, nothing for kids under eight.

That picnic was a big success, on a Sunday in June of 1976, at Rouge Park. There were almost three hundred people that came, workers and their families. It went from before noon to eight in the evening. Some workers brought their grills. People brought bats and baseballs and soccer balls.

When we were organizing it, union leaders spread rumors about it, trying to scare people. They said workers would be fighting each other. It wasn't true, it didn't happen—there was a good feeling among everyone. They liked coming together outside of the plant.

The union leaders also said the picnic was political, that we were playing politics. Yes, that picnic was political because any time workers come together and do something themselves, it's a political move. And the bureaucrats didn't like that!

AT ANOTHER LUNCH TIME meeting, people complained about the way the new line extension had been added. Someone said, "The place is filthy, that's not right. We have to come in here every day." It was also dangerous. The main two elevators in the plant were blocked. Stock was piled in the aisles, blocking it all up and down the aisleway. Someone proposed we do a petition. So we talked about why we were doing it. At the beginning, some workers wanted to criticize the janitors. Others said, "No, the company's responsible. Let them clean it up." Some people thought maybe the union would do something if all of us let the union know that we wanted them to do something. Sometimes the bureaucrats do something when workers let them know they are upset. Anyway, we got three hundred and forty-seven people to sign that petition, almost all our district, plus the hi-lo drivers and people from other districts. I warned people that wasn't enough. So some of the workers who signed it took it into the union office to let the officials know how they felt.

The Local didn't respond. So we decided at another lunch time meeting to send our petition to OSHA. That was June of 1976. OSHA did an inspection in August. It said Chrysler was in violation of health and safety matters and ordered the company to correct things. But it only fined Chrysler one dollar!

The government ends up following in the footsteps of what the big companies want. It's their government, their policy. And some of us knew that. But it was worth doing that anyway. Workers have to be in these plants, every day their whole working lives. It makes a difference that workers decide to speak out. When you don't, you're giving up.

For a little period after OSHA cited Chrysler, the company kept it a bit cleaner. And workers could see that it happened only because they did speak up.

THERE WAS A FOREMAN we called Lead Dog. How he got that name was funny. There was a guy on the fifth floor— one day, he told us, "Man, that little sucker, man, he just like a lead dog." We came up with the idea to get somebody to draw one of those hound dogs, and we took some flyers with that drawing around the plant and put the supervisor's name on it. Flyers all in the cars, flyers on his desk. We put extras in the car and guys would grab them out of the car and put them on the walls, "Lead Dog." A picture of a dog on a leash. So we'd call him that, Lead Dog.

He did not like it. One of the other supervisors down the line in the next group had one of the flyers and was showing it to him. He said, "What you laughing about? It ain't funny! Wait till they stick your name on one!"

LEAD DOG

Lead Dog, Dodge Main foreman

ANOTHER SUPERVISOR, the one who laughed at Lead Dog, had me working on a job that was unsafe. I had to step off the boardwalk, step down about a foot, come across a moving chain, go over there, step up on the boardwalk, get a dashboard, a whole dashboard, step back down, bring that dashboard back across the moving chain, step back up and hook that dashboard into the car. You are coming across the line, the cars are moving, and you've got to cross in between, carrying a heavy piece of stock. It wasn't safe, and that sucker knew it.

I was supposed to be a floater, working on different jobs, but he put me on that job and told me, "Every day you come in, that's going to be your job."

Well, I decided that it wasn't going to be my job. The next day, I tripped and fell. I was coming across the line, carrying this big old dashboard. I fell just where I had to step down over the chain and go between the cars. I went down just like that with that big panel, hit the boardwalk with the big panel and made a lot of noise. Everyone was looking. I got up pretty fast because if I didn't the cars would've run over me.

I told them to call the steward and the safety man. The other workers told the safety man I was almost run over.

He said, "Well, I guess we will have to reorganize this. The company will have to bring this stock over here, so you don't have to be coming through here with that big piece."

So now this guy who laughed at Lead Dog before, now he was angry. The workers were laughing at him. He told Lead Dog, "Well, you can have him back, he's coming back down there."

Lead Dog said, "No, no, no, better send him back to where he came from!"

So that's how I got myself sent back to my old district.

DOWN THERE, in my old district, they put me on the sunroof line. Sunroof was a little line off the main line where they put the car's sunroof in. The line goes around, you put seven or eight, nine cars on the line, they go around and you push them off, then push them over to where they go onto the regular line. When I was working back there, I had people organized to the point that if I wasn't there, they would keep track of the supervisor, write it all down. He'd be doing a worker's job instead of calling for a relief man or a floater to fill in.

When I came back, I'd tell him what he'd done. I read it all off a piece of paper the other workers gave me.

"How did you know, you wasn't even here."

"No, I wasn't here, but somebody was here."

I wasn't a steward, but I was getting people to keep on top of him. I talked to the people around me. "Write it down when something happens. If anyone's around, let them know too. Any violation of the contract, write it down, put the time down, everything he did."

I wasn't a steward, but we got workers to be acting like line stewards. Keeping track of the supervisors. And the supervisors didn't like that. Uhn-uh! No, no!

IN THE SUMMER OF 1976, with the contract coming up, the foremen went on a rampage. One foreman spat in the face of a steward representing a suspended worker. When he pushed the steward, the steward pushed back, and Chrysler fired the steward.

Another foreman was harassing almost everyone in his district. He was one of those guys used to be a militant—until he got a supervisor's job. We called him Road Runner. I don't know where Road Runner was from, he may have been from the South somewhere. Anyway, he was working for the company, doing what the company wanted.

He was putting workers on new jobs, then wrote them up as soon as they couldn't do them. He was a real hatchet man. One day, he was messing with a guy, messing with some worker. The worker picked up something and came at that foreman.

That foreman took off running. That's how he got that name we gave him, the Road Runner. Somebody drew up a cartoon of that doggone Road Runner trying to get away, and we put that up on the board. We were all laughing at him.

Road Runner, Dodge Main foreman

SOME BLACK WORKERS thought that when they got black supervisors, it would be better. But when they got them, they saw it wasn't no better. It was still the company's policies. Some of those supervisors would do whatever the company wants, whatever their boss wants. They knew it wasn't right. But they did it anyway. Sometimes it was worse. Some of those black supervisors were thinking, "I can do that job better than those white supervisors." They wanted to show the boss how tough they were. Just like an Uncle Tom. Just like the Road Runner.

THERE WERE a lot of white supervisors who were rotten. They were all following company policy, doing what the company wanted: keep the workers under control, push the speed-up, get rid of workers. And a lot of them had a racist attitude. You could read it. Maybe they didn't call you "nigger," but they were acting the same way as the ones who did that.

I had a white supervisor down there like that. When I went home, I'd sit down and think about what I could do with him. I was not going to go in there and do nothing back when there's a supervisor like that. When I got up in the morning, I would have thought of something overnight, what I could do, what I am going to do when I go in.

I forget what we called this guy. But I was working, called him over, "Hey man, come here, come over here." He didn't know what I was calling him for. I was just sitting there in the car, sitting down, pushing that rubber molding around the edges of a sunroof. While I was doing that, I said, "Hey, man, you know last night I had a dream." He looked at me. I waited. Then I went on, "Man, I dreamed someone took a shotgun and blowed you away, man." I just went on doing my job and smiled. He got that uncomfortable look. I know that put something on his mind.

Some of those supervisors act crazy toward people, trying to push workers around. You have to let them know that if they act crazy, you'll act crazy. Otherwise, they just go on being a bully.

THAT WAS AROUND the time that Hayward Brown was put on trial again in Detroit. The cops had been after Hayward Brown for quite a while, ever since he and two other young guys, John Boyd and Mark Bethune, were in a shootout with some Detroit cops at the end of 1972. Hayward Brown was put on trial the first time in 1973. The jury must have believed him when he said the cops had attacked the three of them, that they shot back in self-defense. Because the jury acquitted him. But the other two guys were already dead. The cops killed them down in Atlanta somewhere. Shot them down like dogs.

While they were looking for all three of those guys in

Detroit, the cops went around terrorizing people, kicking their doors in. Even a preacher's house, they kicked his door in. One guy was killed when cops burst in his house. That's one reason people supported Hayward Brown, they could see what the cops were doing.

And a lot of people said that Boyd, Brown and Bethune were robbing dope dealers to get them out of the neighborhood. People thought that if someone took the dope houses' money, maybe they would leave. People wanted those dope houses out of their neighborhood. Some guys that called themselves Black Panthers had been doing that before, robbing the dope houses.

People understood that the cops were working with the dope dealers. They saw that every day. And that's why they supported Hayward Brown. He was maybe doing something illegal by robbing, but he was robbing dope houses. And people saw the cops working with these dope dealers at the time. People knew that, and that's why Hayward Brown got a lot of support. The cops kept arresting him and the city would put him on trial, but they couldn't get him convicted. Ten or twelve times, they tried to set him up. But they only convicted him once.

They finally killed Hayward Brown over on the East Side in 1984. People said that an informant for the police lured him to a dope house and someone killed him there. Whatever happened, the cops were behind it. They wanted him dead. They'd been jamming him up all that time, ten years, more than ten years.

When I was working at Dodge Main on the sunroofs, maybe sometime in 1976, we were talking about him. Maybe there was another trial or something that put him in the news. A friend of mine, lived in the same building I did, she and her sister knew some of his family personally. I didn't, but they used to live in the same neighborhood where he grew up.

CHRYSLER WAS ALWAYS pressing people, but when a foreman and a worker got into it, it was always supposed to be the worker's fault. But we could see what was happening. That's why we went to court to defend a couple of workers who got into fights with foremen. We always tried to defend them because if any worker has a problem, we should stand with him. Whatever they did, the company had done worse.

The company sets the rules. The supervisors can do just about what they want to do. They start it. But if the worker does something back, the worker is wrong. The worker is always wrong.

Joe was a relief man who worked on the fourth floor near where I worked. He had fought in Viet Nam. He'd been through stress. Joe told me one day he was hearing the bass from the boom box. It was making him think he was back in Viet Nam. Boom! Boom! It was like something blowing up.

Anyway the supervisor was messing with Joe. I think he was trying to pick Joe off his job, give his relief job to somebody else. Joe told him he wasn't giving up his job, and he had the seniority to keep it. The supervisor was going to go ahead and do it anyway. They had some words, and the supervisor got up in Joe's face, it had got to that point.

So Joe cut him.

The supervisor went toward medical and they took him to the hospital. Joe left the plant and went home. The cops were there, with guns drawn on his wife, waiting for him. They arrested him.

Joe had a family, and he was a vet. I don't think he had a record. Most of the time with someone like that, when there's a fight, they just put him on probation, a suspended sentence. But Chrysler pressed the issue in Joe's case, to make an example. Chrysler wanted Joe charged with attempted murder.

We got involved. We put out a leaflet about Joe's case and went around collecting money for him. We gave the money to his wife. We also went to the court hearings, and there was a crowd of us there, we packed the courtroom. Finally they knocked it down to an assault charge. Even so, he did three years, I think. After he came out, someone told me he worked on the West Side in a barber shop.

There was another case, maybe a year after Joe. Chrysler put another worker out, saying he attacked a supervisor. That was Naji. The supervisor put his hand on Naji and started pushing him. Naji pushed back, so Chrysler fired Naji and the Hamtramck police charged him with assault. We supported Naji, and people gave money for him too.

And we went to court on that, for Naji. Arab workers were there, but some other workers also, a few blacks and a few whites. Packed the doggone little courtroom, right there in Hamtramck. We put out a leaflet calling for workers to support Naji. So we went down there for that, we had it organized, saying, "We have to stand behind this brother."

They dropped the charges down, and he didn't do any time.

FOREMEN WERE always harassing women. Some of those company little boys always seemed to feel they were irresistible and women should fall all over them. But a lot of the women at Dodge Main were fed up with the sex games the foremen played. I heard one woman tell one of those fools, "I come in here to do my job, working for my paycheck just like everyone else. If I wanted to play games, I wouldn't be here, I would stay home." Many of those women said they had a family responsibility, that's why they were in the plant, not because they were looking for a boss who wants them to go along with his sex games.

IT WASN'T JUST the foremen. A lot of guys, regular workers, were saying stupid things to women. A woman came to me about one guy and asked me to say something to him.

When I said something to him about how he was acting, he said, "Man, who wears the pants in your house?"

I said, "What's that got to do with who wears the pants? If she's right, she's right."

When you come to understand the system and if you want to change the system, you have to understand that it's a problem, the attitudes a lot of men have toward women. From what I saw, it wasn't right. We are all working people.

I had to set an example to some of the militant guys in the plant who acted this way. These guys understood that I knew how to fight. I had got into some fights and they knew it. I had to let them know they were wrong how they acted toward women.

IT DIDN'T TAKE LONG before they suspended me on the sunroof line. The Road Runner was the acting general foreman at the time.

My supervisor told me I had to push the car from the main line to the sunroof line. There were supposed to be two workers to do that. You had to push the car sitting on a rolling platform off the regular line, make a turn and come across the aisleway and up onto the sunroof line. But they didn't put a second person on it. That supervisor would come over and be the second person. He wasn't supposed to be doing a worker's job. But Chrysler was trying to cut down on the number of workers.

One day, I spoke out to him: "That's a worker's job. We got a contract, that's a worker's job. A supervisor ain't supposed to be doing it."

So he told me to do it myself, without any second person.

"That's not my job, that's two people's jobs."

He went to tell the Road Runner, and Road Runner came back there hollering about me not doing my job.

I said, "Well, you see, I am doing my job, but if you are

talking about that second job over there, I ain't doing that one, but I am doing my job."

So he suspended me. I was off a week or so, maybe two weeks. Then they called me back.

Any time you are a problem for the company, they definitely try to figure out a way to get rid of you, but especially if you are trying to organize the workers to stand together. And that's where I was coming from. It wasn't just me they wanted out of there. They didn't want workers getting together. Get someone like me out of there, they don't have to worry as much about the other workers. That's what they always do, try to get rid of the workers that other workers look to.

WHEN I CAME BACK, I was put on the third floor. They told me I couldn't even be on the fourth floor! Even on my break or lunch, I couldn't go up there and talk to anyone. I could go outside the plant on my lunch, but not up on the fourth floor.

This was when they were beginning to push the speed-up. They tell you to do something, and you do it, then it gets to be part of your job. That's how they get rid of workers. They trick someone into doing more, then get rid of someone else.

So I was steady discussing with people, "If it ain't right, why do it?"

THE NEXT LOCAL election at Dodge Main came up in 1977. I thought about running for steward again, but when I talked to workers around me, they thought maybe I should run for president. I thought about it. People had talked about my case a lot—about them removing me and about the way the union handled it—people who were in that district, but also in some other districts. They knew about what happened and they supported me. I didn't know if I could win, but running for president gave me a bigger opening to expand what I stood for, not just with the workers in my district, but throughout the plant.

Probably I could have won for steward, but I didn't need to be the steward to be organizing workers in the area. I was already doing that, anyway.

So I campaigned through the whole plant. Workers on the east side of the plant, they didn't even know me. They came in and came out the other end of the plant, and I never saw them. They might have heard some people talk about me, but they didn't know me. But because I was free to go around campaigning, I had a chance to meet them. And I could talk to them. The rest of the time I couldn't do that.

Most of what I took on was the policy of the union, what a union should be doing, what the UAW wasn't doing. Even back then in the 1970s, we were going backwards. You could see it. The leaders of the union weren't challenging things. A lot of workers even then were thinking there was something the union leaders weren't doing they should be doing. When workers talked to me, they heard something totally different from what they were hearing from these guys in office.

One day, a bunch of workers were with me, campaigning in front of the plant. I had a bullhorn, saying, "We don't need a company president, we need a union president." Workers went by laughing when they heard that—even one of the guys on the Executive Board was smiling about that one.

I know Joe Davis and other officers were worried I might win even if I didn't know people in some parts of the plant. He was running for president. They didn't know what people might do. And they heard people talking about what I was saying. So the bureaucrats were really pushing.

One friend of mine, Jackie, was always out there campaigning with us. Joe Davis kept coming at her down on her job. Finally she just backed up and said, "Well, I'm not having nothing to do with elections then." She talked to other people about what had happened, and she was still supporting me. But she wasn't really out campaigning like she was going to do. And I don't think she even voted. I think that happened with some other people, who probably didn't go to vote at all because they were worried about what could happen to them.

It was a two-day election, but they didn't let my challenger in to monitor the voting on the first day. They could mess with the votes for one whole day. We knew something rotten could happen. But even I was surprised that they would be that open.

I didn't win, and I didn't even make it into the run-off. But I think it was worth doing. It was a means of talking to the workers, saying what needed to be said.

Some of the militant workers were disappointed and they got pissed at the other workers. "Those lying ass so and so's, they didn't even show up." The militant workers had talked to everyone around them. They heard everyone say they were going to vote for me, but not all of the others even came out to vote.

That's so normal for that to happen. But those militant workers were thinking we were going to win, and it didn't happen. Then they started getting it in their mind that it's not worth doing anything because nothing's ever going to happen.

I tried to talk to them about that. I wanted them to understand what workers can do, even if they aren't doing it now. I wanted them to get a bigger picture. I tried to talk to them about what the bigger problems are, about the capitalist system. We are going to have to know what that system is if we are going to deal with our problems.

MY DAUGHTER wanted to come visit me, her daddy. Her name was Sammie Louise, but we called her Lulu. Her momma talked to me, wanted to know if it was OK. I said, sure. So that summer of 1977, Lulu came and stayed with me. She was 14.

Sam's daughter Lulu not long after her first visit to Detroit

I used to talk to Lulu sometimes on the phone, and I would send her money for things she wanted, but that was the first time I saw her since I left L.A. She was only four years old when I left.

When I picked her up at the airport, she seemed glad to see me. I was glad to see her too. I don't think she'd been on a plane before.

I was working then, second shift, nights, so I was gone a lot, and it wasn't good for her to stay at my place by herself. She didn't grow up around there and didn't know anyone. All she was doing was sitting there by herself.

My sister-in-law Grace said, "Bring her over here, let her stay over here." So most of the time she stayed over with Grace. My two nieces were close to her age, and she liked that better anyway. Faye was just about the same age; Annette was about three years older. They all hung out together that summer.

I'd see her just about every day because I'd go over there before I went to work. Sometimes I'd take her shopping so she could buy a few little things she wanted.

Lulu didn't seem to be in any hurry to go home. She had family she didn't know before, not just me, but my nieces and my nephews. So she was learning from them. And I talked to her about things she didn't know about, like how to protect herself if she was having any kind of sex. She wasn't ready to start taking care of a kid, but I could see she was out there with some of the boys.

She ended up staying the whole summer. After she went back, she used to call me more than she did before, and we talked about different things.

Twenty-Two
Plant Closings, Layoffs, Fight to Get Back

THEY STARTED TALKING about closing Dodge Main in 1978. They began to put people out of there. It was 10,000 workers when I got there in 1970. Finally, they got most of us out of there in '79, maybe in the fall. They didn't close everything until 1980, but there wasn't any production going on after 1979. Only skilled trades tearing down the machinery.

That's the first time I saw something like that, a plant closing. And Dodge Main wasn't the last. It was just the beginning. I guess that happened before, in the 1950s, a lot of plants closing. But I didn't see that before.

All those people laid off—a lot of them were not going to get back to work, and if they did, not back in auto. That's when the numbers in auto began to drop, and drop some more. There were people who didn't have many years, didn't have much seniority when auto started laying off. They were left there out in the street. There were a lot of people out of work in Detroit for years.

SOME OF US had come to Dodge Main from Lynch Road or Jefferson. We were signed up to go back to our home plants. So I ended up back at Lynch Road.

I wasn't back there very long before Chrysler came back, saying it needed concessions. They wanted to cut out our wage increase, freeze our wages for three years, get rid of COLA. Chrysler said it would go bankrupt if they didn't get it.

Workers heard UAW president Doug Fraser on TV saying that he wouldn't stand for a three-year wage freeze. But he also said workers would have to give up something.

Chrysler used the government and the union to push that contract on us. Congress threatened to let Chrysler go bankrupt unless workers gave up something. And union leaders said it was just temporary, we'd get it all back as soon as things picked up.

Some workers thought they already sacrificed too much with the layoffs. They didn't want to give up anything more. But finally people voted for the 1980 concessions. They didn't see they had any choice. They thought they would lose their jobs if they didn't vote to cut their own wages.

WE LOST OUR JOBS anyway. In 1981, Chrysler closed Lynch Road. And it closed other plants too, stamping plants.

Just before we got laid off, workers were talking about sabotaging. They wanted to mess up production on the line, destroy everything. Some of those people had just left Dodge Main, not but a year or so before, so they were pissed off when Chrysler started talking about closing Lynch Road too. Some of the black workers were talking, "We're gonna burn that motherfucker down." Workers were talking all that kind of stuff. A lot of the workers started doing things right away, just some minor stuff. But there was some real sabotage, too. That didn't happen much at Dodge Main, but you could see it at Lynch Road. Those workers were going to be put out in the street again, no job, and they were mad.

I WAS LAID OFF then from early 1981 to August of '84. More than three years. I saw Chrysler pick up other workers that had less time than I had. After a year, they were working.

Chrysler found jobs for them somewhere. I guess by that time Chrysler decided it didn't want me. Maybe I had raised enough hell at Dodge Main and Lynch Road.

I put in a complaint. The company finally tried to send me out to Trenton. That was over thirty miles away. I refused. I asked, "What's wrong with all these jobs in Detroit? People that were sent to Jefferson got much less time than I got, and you want to send me out to Trenton?"

"Well you don't have to go out there, but we don't have anything right now. We'll have to put you on the list to call."

"Well put me on the list then." I wasn't ready to make that trip back and forth every day.

My papers were at Jefferson, but they didn't pick me up there. They sent me to other plants. The guy at Mack Stamping said, "Why did they send you out here? We got people laid off got more time than you got." He called Personnel at Warren Truck, where Jefferson sent my papers.

"Oh, it must have been a mistake. Send him up here."

So I went up to the Truck Plant. They sent me to Mound Road, the Engine Plant. There wasn't nothing happening there. Nope. They sent me to four or five places. None of them had a place for me.

Then they sent me to the Stamping Plant on Nine Mile. That's part of Chrysler too. At the Nine Mile Stamping Plant, they put me through a physical, okayed me for work. One of the nurses even said to me, "Oh, the party's over now," expecting they would put me back to work. But then I went to Personnel. The man in Personnel started pulling out my papers. "Looking at your medical records," he said, "you had back problems, and this is heavy work in here, you won't be able to do this work here." He tried to get me to sign some papers.

"No," I told him, "I'm not signing nothing. When I left out of Lynch Road, I was working the assembly line, heavy work. I'm not signing nothing." I wasn't going to sign off, saying I was OK with it.

"Well," he said, "you'll just have to go back on unemployment then. They should be calling you from Truck, they're putting on another line."

But they didn't call me. They had a plan not to put me back to work.

So I went up to Truck, where my papers were. A guy working in Personnel, a guy I knew from another plant, said, "I'm just going to be frank with you, man. They are not going to put you to work here." He told me that straight out. That let me know they were just messing me around. They were running a scam, running me around to all these plants.

LULU'S BROTHER Donald came to visit me one summer when I was still out of work. That was the first time I saw him too since I left. He was 16 or 17, older than Lulu was when she came. He knew she came, so he wanted to come stay too.

I was laid off, so he could stay with me, but I took him over to my sister-in-law's house, too. She had two sons a year or two younger than him, Greg and Mannering. Four doors down from me there was a family with a lot of kids. He got to know a couple of them, young boys his age, and he hung out with them.

Most of the time, we got along OK.

But sometimes, he was trying to be a little tough guy, and there were some problems.

One day when I was gone, he was at the house. He took my shotgun, showing off with these boys down the street.

I had showed him how to use that gun, in case someone came in the house when I wasn't there, so he would know what to do. I showed him what to do, how to be careful with it, not to take it out in the street. But that's what he did.

The guy who lived downstairs from me told me, "I saw your boy, he had a shotgun, down the street with it, with those boys."

When I caught Donald up about that, he said, "It was that boy's BB gun."

My neighbor said, "That wasn't no BB gun. It was your shotgun."

I told Donald, "Do NOT put your hands on my gun again. Definitely do NOT take it out of the house." That was the end of that.

I noticed my phone bill was going up. And Lulu called me and told me he was calling everybody he knew. She knew I was laid off.

I had to tell him he couldn't be using my phone like that. Long distance calls, calling everyone he knew, talking every day, all day long. He'd be getting my phone cut off. I was laid off and I couldn't keep paying that bill.

So he cut back. Maybe he still called a little bit, but not like before.

Donald was looking around at what the other kids were wearing, the shoes they had. He wanted some just like that, thirty-five or forty-dollar gym shoes back then. I was paying fifteen for mine. You know how these young boys are. They see advertising for these shoes. The first thing they want is to get them. They don't have the money. But some boy gets them, and that makes the other ones want them.

We went and got some shoes for him, twenty-some dollars. But not the ones he wanted. I told him I couldn't get him those he wanted. "I don't have the money." I was only just getting unemployment checks then.

I guess I was going through what parents run into all the time. And that was just for the summer.

One day we went to a picnic. It must have been a Local picnic, a plant reunion for Dodge Main. Donald and me were with this young guy I knew from Dodge Main. We started running, racing—and they both beat me.

When I told Lulu about it on the phone, she was surprised.

"What?" She was on the track team in school, and she told me she used to beat Donald. She couldn't believe it, "You let Donald beat you?"

I had to say, "Yeah, he beat me."

One day we were going visiting. We were in this restaurant, some place on the turnpike, and we saw Muhammad Ali. People were around him, talking to him. Ali was one of the most popular boxers, and people still remembered that he had gone to jail because he wouldn't go fight in that war in Viet Nam. He talked against it.

I told Donald, "That's Muhammad Ali." We went over to where he was and talked with him for a minute. I told him we were glad to see him. "Donald is visiting me for the summer. He's from Southern California, and I live in Detroit now and he wanted to see you." Muhammad Ali said he was touring. I don't remember where he said he was going.

You could see from Donald's expression, he was proud to meet Muhammad Ali. You know he was going to go talk to his friends, tell them, "I met Muhammad Ali."

I WAS STILL OFF in 1982. That was the year the UAW leadership negotiated a new contract, and the Chrysler workers were upset. They thought they were supposed to get back what they gave up in the 1980 concessions contract— and they didn't get it.

Chrysler kept me out, so I had the time to get around, talk to workers at other plants, get them involved. If I was on the job, I wouldn't have time to do that. I went to different plants, Jefferson, the Truck Plant, went up to Sterling plants, Stamping. I knew workers at all those plants. Ten thousand workers used to be at Dodge Main, and some of them went to those plants.

We passed out information, called on the workers to vote it down. We stood in front of the gate at Jefferson, talking, and we had meetings near the plant. Workers came out to hear about the contract. I had known some of those people, had worked together with them at Dodge Main, and they remembered me.

There was a meeting in the Local 212 hall. I don't remember how it happened, but Jefferson workers were meeting at Local 212. There were about a thousand people in that hall. It was packed. And people were angry about the new contract because it didn't give them back what they gave up in the 1980 concessions. There were microphones set up, and we lined up to talk.

When I got up there to the mike, someone said, "You don't work here, you don't have a right to speak."

"I'm a laid off worker, UAW. I have questions about that contract. And I have just as much right to speak as any one of you up there."

The International reps were sitting up on the stage. They had someone pull the plug on the microphone. A lot of people started yelling, "Let him speak." Workers were so fed up they began to walk out of that meeting. They already knew they were going to vote against it.

I went out to Dodge Truck. I was passing out a leaflet against that contract with workers I knew there. We were calling on the other workers, "Let's go, let's shut the whole damn thing down." We were on the lot, so the security guard came out to see what we were doing. He had got one of the leaflets, I think, and showed his boss. He told me I had to leave, I didn't work there, couldn't be on the parking lot.

"What do you mean, I can't be on the parking lot? I done worked at Chrysler, and then I'm laid off, and my record is in the Truck Plant too, and all the concessions I gave to keep this plant afloat and keep this company afloat and I can't be on the parking lot? You gonna say I ain't got the right?" I told him, "I got more right to be on this parking lot than YOU have."

Back he came, "When you see that little black and white

come out, the police coming around the corner, I guess you'll leave."

"Well, get on the phone then. I ain't going nowhere."

He went back and told his little boss. I saw them standing there, talking. I was still passing out flyers, and there were four or five workers standing around me, wanting to know what was going on. The security was looking at us, but they didn't call the police, they let it go. So I finished passing out the leaflet.

I went to other plants with people I knew. I went to Sterling, I knew some workers who were out there because after they closed Lynch Road and Dodge Main, they sent some of these people to Sterling. So we passed out those leaflets there.

And other Chrysler workers were organizing too.

Chrysler said it had no more money. It couldn't give us anything more. And UAW president Doug Fraser said that contract was the best workers could get.

But when the vote came, Chrysler workers voted that contract down. That was something big. That was the first time since World War II it ever happened that a national contract was voted down.

Seven weeks later, Chrysler came back with a new contract. They gave us a little something. We didn't get back what we lost two years before. But we made them come up with something, more than what they said they could.

So maybe Chrysler made a mistake keeping me out all those months. They gave me time to get around and work against that contract.

I GOT MY HIGH SCHOOL DIPLOMA while I was out of work. I went back to school to Northern High School in Detroit, maybe a couple of years. The school wasn't all day, just certain classes in the late afternoon. The whole room was filled, almost like a regular class. We took some math, some science classes, and English classes, maybe some history. Most of the people there were younger than me. But there were some people my age. I was in my forties.

I went to Highland Park Community College to take the test. There were three or four parts of the test that I didn't get to. We were timed and I wasn't fast enough. But the parts I finished I think I got about 90%. So I had a high enough score to pass it, and I got a GED.

I came out of a segregated school in Alabama that didn't give us much education. And I just dropped out, went right into a job. So I had some problems. But all the things I had been doing and all the things I had been reading put me back on track.

CHRYSLER SAID MY BACK was a problem. That was their excuse for keeping me out. They said I had back injuries. But my back injuries were job related. I injured my back in the plant twice, and I was out on workers' comp because of those injuries in the plant, once for a couple of months, once for a couple of weeks.

Sometime in 1982, I got a comp lawyer, an older guy who had been around a while, Morton Eden. When he looked at the record, he asked me, "They don't want you because of your back injuries? Those are plant related. Hell, if they can't find you some work you can do, then they're going to have to pay you workers' comp." So he ran that right back on them, "If you can't find nothing that he can do, well put him on workers' comp because the injury was done inside the plant."

But Chrysler turned us down. We had to appeal. They turned that down. We went to a hearing. By that time, it was April 1983. Chrysler got that hearing put off for more than a year. Finally in May '84, there was a new hearing. In June, the workers' comp judge ordered Chrysler to pay me for all the time I was off, over three years, and the judge ordered

Chrysler to pay me a weekly comp check from then on unless they brought me back. And they had to pay my lawyer, too.

Just like that, Chrysler decided I could do the work after all. Heavy work, too. They sent me one or two comp checks, then called me to the McGraw Glass Plant.

Twenty-Three
Into McGraw—and "Out on Wyoming"

I WENT TO CHRYSLER'S McGraw plant in August 1984. I hadn't been there a month, when one of the Local union leaders stopped by. He said, "I already heard about you, that you're going to be a problem." I just let it go.

I already knew a few people at McGraw—some from Dodge Main, some from Lynch, not too many, maybe about thirty people or so. There was one guy I knew at Dodge Main, Gimbu, who came over about that same time. He was one of those people who would stand up to the foremen.

And I was talking to McGraw workers, especially after I'd been there a few months. That was enough to get a workers newsletter started right there. The first one at McGraw came out in January of 1985. Some people already knew about the "Spark" newsletter from other plants. But it was new to some people.

It didn't take long before people were telling me things that should go in.

If they had something going on down where they were working, they would let me know. They just came to where I worked and let me know. Sometimes I went around to get some information from people I knew. I'd tell them, "The newsletter's coming out."

In the morning, there would be someone at the gate passing out the newsletter. But he couldn't get that many out because he was giving it to people who were driving cars past him. They were running forty miles an hour on Wyoming before they turned into that gate. And they were in a hurry sometimes because they were late. The company wouldn't let him stand inside the gate. As soon as he did, the guard came out, told him he couldn't be on Chrysler property. But we got those newsletters around inside.

When I first got there, I was careful about what I did. I used to take a bunch of newsletters in there, put them on the restroom doors and different places.

When I took them in the cafeteria, I didn't have them open. I put them in a folded-up Free Press, laid that on the table. That was the morning newspaper. Someone would pick the Free Press up, and there would be the newsletters. They'd fall on the table, and people would come over and pick them up. They went fast.

Some people came by to pick up some little packs of newsletters from me at a gas station close to McGraw. But the owner kept watching me to see what I was doing. One day, I went in the station and saw this Arab guy I knew from Dodge Main. He said something about me to the Arab owner of the station, "Sam's not no problem. He's a good guy. I've been knowing him for years. We worked at another plant together."

So then the Arab guys in the station got to know me, and I used the station as a place to meet workers from McGraw who stopped there to get a few newsletters to take in.

After a while, I used to put the newsletters out where people first came in. Someone would see them, take some for other people and let others know, "The Spark's here."

One day, a foreman grabbed that whole pile. I saw him from where I was working and I yelled at him, "That's a newsletter for the workers, not for the company. Put them back." I guess he was surprised. But he put them back.

The "Spark" newsletter was coming out regular, every couple weeks. So sometimes we'd collect money to pay for the newsletter and support the "Spark." When people gave me the money, I'd write their name down and how much money they gave, and put their money in the envelope. Sometimes, they wrote their name down. Sometimes, I just put a number down, because I didn't know their name. I had a big brown envelope I put the names on. They could all see I kept a record of the money they donated. I still have a few of those envelopes. One from August 1998 had ninety-four people's names on it. We collected money to support the "Spark" every few months or so. Some people gave to the guy at the gate, but that wasn't too easy either, with cars rushing by.

When people picked up that newsletter and read it, they got something different than what they heard from the union and the company. And it brought people around me who liked that newsletter. Some of them gave money for it, took it around, and talked to me about things to go in it.

IN THE FALL OF 1985, there was a short strike at Chrysler. Before the strike started, some of us talked about what would happen. In August, a few people signed a statement with me and got it around, calling on everyone to be active in the strike. It said: "We need strong picket lines. We need to let other workers know about our strike. We need to keep in contact with other Chrysler workers."

We knew what the top union leaders were going to do, knew it from what they'd been doing in the past. They'd take the workers out to make it seem like they would make a fight, even while they were making deals with the company. But they wouldn't organize a real strike, just small little picket lines. After a couple weeks, they'd come back and say

THE SPARK

INCREASED PROFITS — OR JOBS FOR ALL?

GM has announced its plans for the future: the Saturn plants. And what GM has announced, every other company is preparing to do: other auto companies, other industrial companies, all those other workplaces -- offices, hospitals, government services -- which try to push their workers as hard as the assembly line pushes GM workers.

Saturn supposedly will mean better quality, less inventory, more worker participation, more robots, more attention paid to engineering design, etc. etc. etc. Look behind all the fine words, and what it boils down to is that GM expects to reduce the number of workers to 1/2 or even 1/3 of today's work force.

Undoubtedly, some of the increased productivity will come from the added machinery, robots, etc. But a bigger share will come from speed-up, plain and simple -- in exactly the same way that the auto industry -- and every other industry -- has pushed the workers, during the last ten years, to produce more and more.

Saturn will mean fewer jobs in the better paying industries, and more jobs in the low paid services, and more workers without any hopes of a job. Just like today. Today, after 2 years of so-called economic recovery, the unemployment rate stands at better than 7% -- a figure that in the past would have been seen only in a recession. And a bigger and bigger share of those "lucky" enough to have jobs are working at a McDonalds or a car wash for minimum wages. Tomorrow, we can expect to see even more minimum wage jobs and a 10 or even 15% unemployment rate -- when the economy is booming.

According to the bosses, it's reasonable, it's the only way to go.

But it's not true!

If more machinery and robots make each worker more productive, if each worker works harder, if all this means that the same number of workers can produce much more, why get rid of workers? Why not reduce the number of hours we all have to work? Everyone could have the same number of cars, houses, clothing, food, and all the other things we need. The increased productivity of each worker would allow us to produce the same or more, to fulfill all the needs of society, and still to work less time. That is, to work less time, but still make the same weekly wages. The higher hourly wages could come out of our increased productivity.

It's perfectly reasonable. Much more reasonable than what GM and the other bosses propose.

This is the question. How is the workers' increased productivity to be used?

If we leave things to the bosses, it will be used in the same way it has been over the last 10 years, to push up the bosses' profits, while more of us have low paid jobs or no jobs at all.

If the workers want to use the increased productivity for themselves, they will have to turn their backs on what the bosses want.

The workers will have to fight to impose their wishes on the bosses, just as the bosses have imposed their wishes on us up until now.

celebrate!

SPARK WINTER DINNER & FORUM '85
SUNDAY FEBRUARY 10, 5:30 TO 10 PM
* * * with dinner at 6:30 only * * *

Plan now to come together with other workers from around the area who are concerned about what lies ahead for workers in 1985. There will be a presentation and discussion following the dinner. There are also political and science displays, films, crafts and music for you to enjoy.

$2.25 plus a potluck dish covers the cost for the full dinner and evening, but tickets must be bought ahead. So buy one at the gate soon, or through friends. Don't miss it.

Spark newsletter McGraw, side 1, 1985

Sam Johnson

Write to: McGraw SPARK
P.O. Box 1047, Detroit, MI 48231

WORK THE OVERTIME OR TAKE BACK THE CONCESSIONS

You can understand why so many people are pressed to work the overtime. Because we can always use the money. But if we are pressed to work the overtime, it could be that we are underpaid.

Right now, we are making $1.25 an hour less than GM and Ford workers. And if we go back a few years, the money we gave up in concessions would come to more than $2 an hour. This would average out to around $90 a week more we would have if only Chrysler had given us back what is due to us. We wouldn't be pressed in the same way to work the overtime.

If Chrysler had only given it back -- or if we had only fought to take it back.

NO STANDARD -- GO SLOW

Work standards still haven't been set on a lot of jobs. It's been almost a half year now. So, how long could it possibly take to set a work standard?

Of course, if they were set, it doesn't mean they would be reasonable. And it doesn't mean Chrysler wouldn't try to violate them.

But when Chrysler refuses even to set a standard, it shows that the company is trying to push for every possible bit of production it can wring out of us.

So the workers can't be blamed if they try the same tactic, only in reverse: work as slow as it's humanly possible to do.

After all, there's no standard set!

SEND THAT FOOL THIS WAY !

Did you hear about the foreman on second shift who spends his time working hourly jobs?

They say he worked himself into a frenzy trying to prove it was possible to work an impossible job. Of course, no one reasonable is convinced by someone making a spectacle of himself!

But a couple of workers got a break for a time while he was carrying on like a fool.

STRESS CAN KILL

A general foreman on first shift died of a heart attack during his lunch break. He was only in his fifties.

There are a lot of things which can contribute to a heart attack. But stress is certainly high up on the list -- especially when someone dies that young.

And stress is what we get in here -- whether someone's in management, or whether they do the work around here. With all the noise, with the constant danger of being cut, and with the constant push for more production -- the plant is one big box of stress.

Each one of us is a candidate for a heart attack. And one of the main reasons is that we work for a company which tries to impose its profits by subjecting us to stress.

ONE-SIDED 1984 ACHIEVEMENT

Last week a lot of workers were given a certificate of achievement for improving quality in production.

In this place, every single worker should have received more than a certificate. Just look at the speed-up and extra work we've had to put up with.

No wonder some of the workers thought the certificate was a big joke.

If Chrysler is serious about wanting quality in production, then management would slow down the pace on all the jobs. Then maybe management would receive its certificate from the workers in 1985.

Please pass this on to a friend.
** **

WATCH NEXT WEEK FOR THE SPARK NEWSPAPER. ON SALE AT THIS PLANT -- 25¢ ONLY -- NEWS FROM THE WORKERS' VIEWPOINT.

Spark newsletter McGraw, side 2, 1985

they did the best they could, and then we'd have concessions again.

We understood this, what the bureaucracy had been doing, so we wanted to prepare people to make a real fight, stop the concessions.

We went around with that statement to talk about what we had to do. And we got names, tried to organize people to come out more often on the picket lines than the union scheduled them for. And more people did come out to the lines. The strike didn't last very long—just long enough to worry people and for the union to push the idea of "co-operation." The big deal was supposed to be new Local contracts, what they called "Modern Operating Agreements." The company wanted to get rid of classifications and work rules. What they wanted was to push people to work harder.

I was active with other people to get that Local contract voted down, some of the same people from the strike. That's when I met Don. He was organizing people against the Local contract. In early December, we voted it down. The Local leaders brought back the same contract a second time in January, pushing it. They said, "The company won't invest any more and the plant will close." But workers voted it down again, this time with seventy-five per cent against, a bigger NO vote than the first time. The company threatened it would close the plant if it didn't get a "yes" vote. Workers voted "no" anyway. The company didn't close. And Chrysler brought in new machinery!

I RAN FOR DELEGATE to the UAW Convention in early 1986. An older McGraw worker said something to a guy working near me: "What's he running for? He just got here."

But I had worked at Chrysler for 18 years. I knew people at a lot of other plants. I didn't know if I could win at McGraw, but I wanted to say something about what was wrong in what the union was doing and what workers could do to change that. At first, the Local didn't put my name on the ballot. I had to get a lawyer to do a quick appeal just to get on the ballot. The Local finally agreed to put me on—six days before the election!

I put out a leaflet with the title: "Not a time to party, but a time to fight." Workers knew that a lot of the people who went to the convention just went to have a big party at the workers' expense. That's why I used that title. I said, "I think we should send people to the UAW Convention who are not afraid of the man, people who are tired of concessions, speed-up and plant closings; people ready to organize a fight to stop the company's attacks.... The UAW leadership's policy has been to accept the concessions, plant closings and worsening working conditions. They said to us there is nothing we can do but go along with the companies."

I told the workers that I knew I couldn't change anything at the UAW Convention by myself, but I said it would make a difference if people like me went.

At McGraw, I knew workers who came from Dodge Main, some Yugoslav guys and Arab guys, and there were some black workers around me. About thirty of us had come there from Dodge Main. And I had been talking to McGraw workers since I got there. Some of the people I knew were talking to other workers for me. But there were a lot of people I didn't know. I got around the whole plant campaigning. I let people know who I was. I introduced myself. If you just put out something, a lot of people don't see you, don't know who you are.

I didn't make it, but I came in tenth out of twenty-one running for four spots, better than a former Local president and my own committeeman and some other well-known people in the Local.

THAT'S ABOUT THE TIME I was suspended by the Snake. Workers told me how that foreman got that name.

He told someone, "If you don't do what I tell you, I'll strike you." Just like a rattlesnake. That's why people gave him that name, the Snake.

So, anyway, the Snake came in our department to take the shift for half a day. I never had a problem with the regular supervisor. But the Snake was something else, and he was just there for half a day.

There were problems with the machinery, so the line was shut down. Some people were going through parts, looking for the bad ones, taking out the good parts and throwing out the scrap. The Snake told me to go over there and work with them. I just got there, and I was talking to them to find out what were they looking for.

The Snake came running around the corner, just that fast. "Why are you standing up? I didn't send you here to stand around, I sent you down here to do some work."

"Wait a minute," I said. "Before you do some work, first you find out what you've got to do."

"Oh, you don't know what you gotta do?"

"No, I don't know what they're doing."

So the Snake said, "OK, you don't know how to do that, I know you know how to do this." He got a broom. "Clean up around the place then. I know you know how to do that."

I got the broom and I swept on back down to where those people were. Most of them were trying to stay away from him, the way he acted. I asked them, "What's the deal on this dude?"

A few minutes later, the Snake came back, told me to get on my machine. I went back, and I started thinking, "I've got to say something to this sucker." When he came around my way, I told him, "Hey, man, look here, I'd like to talk to you. I want to know, why are you acting that way? You don't even much know my name yet. What's wrong with you?"

A new foreman would try to know who the workers are. But he just started in, "I don't HAVE to know your name.

You do what I tell you, or you'll be out on Wyoming." That's the street the plant was on, Wyoming and McGraw. And he went walking off.

He was used to people being afraid around him. You can't go along with bullies. If you don't do something, it's just going to get worse.

When he went by again, I told him, "Hey, man, you're acting tough but I don't think you're all that tough. All I see is a little boy trying to tell a man what to do." The repairman was sitting there, checking it all out. But I wasn't done. "Malcolm X said we still had some houseboys running around here. I'm just trying to be nice. Because the master might've come straight up and said, 'house nigger.' And the way you're acting here, you just may be one."

Oh boy! The repairman had his head down. He was laughing.

The Snake got on the phone and called Labor Relations. They sent the steward down. The Snake told the steward, "I'm suspending this man."

The steward asked, "Why?"

The Snake said, "He insulted me in front of other people."

"What? You can't suspend someone for that. Let's talk."

But the Snake took me and the steward to the office. He got his papers out and his little book trying to find something he could use to write me up.

I told him, "Look man, I just been back to work, I been off for three years and something, and I just been back and I'm telling you, if I don't have a job, you won't have one!" And I hit the damn table, Bam! The people behind the partition, their heads came up.

The Snake said, "You threatened me."

The steward told him, "The man ain't threatened you. There are legal means to cost you your job. He ain't threatened you."

Anyway, they suspended me. They kept me off a couple days, then they brought me back to work. When the grievance went through, I finally got paid for that time I was off. I hadn't done anything. Just said what I thought. It wasn't a big thing, but it pulled some of those guys from McGraw who wanted to fight closer to me. I think that's when I got to know Tom. He was the repairman. He and two other workers signed statements about what happened.

WE WERE TRYING to fight against the speed-up. Workers who had been at McGraw said this was the first time they had a problem with the company steady trying to speed it up, just all the time.

Chrysler had the time study guy trying to see how many seconds it would take you to do each part of your job. Then they'd add something to your job. Their intention was to get more work out of us. Someone hollered at him, "Hey, you think it's so easy? Why don't you come here and see if you can do it in those few seconds? Try it for a day, see how it is."

We would tell different people, "You're going to have to work at a regular pace. If you work this fast, they're going to get rid of someone and you'll be doing two jobs. They won't need all of us if they can get you to do all this work. They'll have you doing one and a half people's jobs, and get rid of one out of three."

One of the guys, he was on the line where I was, he'd be working so fast and then run down the line to get himself a break. I had a talk with him, "Man you better slow down, specially when the time study comes around. They'll have you doing two jobs if they see you can work ahead and go down the line. If they see you rushing, rushing, rushing to run down there and talk to someone else, they'll have you working like that the whole time."

He listened to that, he got it.

Chrysler was trying to speed the line up. In early 1987, McGraw tried to increase the production standard in our department from 1368 pieces of glass in an eight-hour shift to 2058—a fifty per cent increase. They announced it just like that.

But we weren't going for it. The shit was already going fast enough. So we organized people to work at a steady pace. "Don't kill yourself. Just work at a regular pace. If that don't do it, then fuck it."

They wrote some of us up for missing work. They threatened us. But they couldn't get the production they wanted.

I GUESS CHRYSLER got to see that we were a problem. Our foreman was an older guy, getting ready to retire. He said he only had a short time more and he'd be out. We usually got along OK. He wasn't someone who just wrote up workers for no reason. They moved him down to the next department.

They took this other foreman from midnights and made him foreman over our group. When he came in, he told the repairman that he had orders to "clean up" the department. One of the black workers said he had transferred to another shift to get away from him, as rotten as he was toward the black workers. Some workers said he was acting like he was still in the service, the way he gave orders. So someone started calling him Sergeant 60.

Sergeant 60 started in on different people. There was a young black guy in my department. Sergeant 60 just kept on him. The young guy got behind, missed a piece of glass because something was going wrong. Sergeant 60 told him, "I don't want you missing not one more job, not one piece of glass."

But if the machinery isn't working right, you do miss a glass. Something was wrong and the young guy had got

210

in the hole. He was working like crazy to catch up, and he needed help. Instead, Sergeant 60 was standing there, right up on the guy, just standing there, and the guy couldn't even work. Sergeant 60 was all over him.

I told that young guy, "Man, you don't have to put up with that shit, I mean, call the steward, man."

Sergeant 60 hollered, "You ain't got nothing to do with this, I ain't talking to you. You wait till I come after you."

"I do have something to do with it. Any time you're messing with another worker, I got something to do with it. Any time you're messing with the union, you're messing with me."

He was still standing there over that young guy.

I told him: "The way you're acting, all you need now is your whip. Just like a slave driver, you know? All you need is your whip."

Oh, man! He was mad. Sergeant 60 came running over. I don't know how he got over so fast, but he pointed his finger in my face, told me he was going to fire me.

His boss came up behind him, calmed him down.

MAY 1987, there was a steward election. I started talking to people, telling them I was thinking about running for the production workers' steward on day shift. The people who knew me thought it was a good idea.

McGraw was different than Dodge Main. McGraw was right on the edge of Dearborn, and Dearborn was still pretty openly racist. And you felt that in the plant. There was still a real sharp division between white and black.

That was a big thing I tried to talk about in that election. This is still part of the problem with the unions today. That racism's been there, and it's still one of the problems. That's how it was when I came in there, racism and that division. The way I saw it, workers had to get past that.

"Unity means all the workers, that's what makes us

strong"—that's what I tried to say so all the workers could hear that. "Instead of fighting ourselves, we all have to stand together."

Here's something from one of my leaflets in that campaign: "Some workers told me I shouldn't talk about racism, or the white workers won't vote for me. I don't think so. I think some white workers can also see that racism divides us and hurts all of us. But even if it costs me votes, I am going to tell the truth because racism is a division created by the bosses and it stands in the way of working people uniting our power. It stands in the way of a strong union, and it also stands in the way of humanity moving forward."

A lot of black workers were reading that and talking to me about it. Some white workers talked to me, too. Some of them didn't like it, but some did understand.

There were still a lot of people at the other end of the plant I didn't know, but I got into the runoff and I didn't lose by that much. I think it showed that you can speak to the workers about a serious problem, and a lot of them will hear you even when they don't agree.

AUGUST 1987, Chrysler set up a separate company that was called Acustar. Most of Chrysler's parts plants ended up in Acustar. McGraw Glass went in there. Later on, GM did the same, setting up Delphi, and Ford did it with Visteon.

The company and the union announced they wanted Local union agreements for all the Acustar plants like the one we already turned down twice at McGraw. There were eight of us that signed a statement. We used it to go around talking, warning people that Acustar was the first step toward getting rid of the parts plants. And later on, that's what all those companies did. They used those new companies to push lower wages. It was the starting point for Two-Tier. They lowered wages for new hires in the parts plants first. Then they finally brought that Two-Tier into the assembly plants in 2007.

CHRYSLER SET UP to fire me. (Anyway, that's what a jury must have thought. They awarded me quite a bit of money after we took Chrysler to trial for firing me.)

We were out of glass because Sergeant 60 had the set-up man working over on the other side, lying down under the machinery, trying to fix something. We were waiting on the glass, the woman who worked with me, Catherine, and me. We didn't know the set-up man was nearby; we couldn't see him. And we didn't see the supervisor.

Sergeant 60 came over, yelling, "What the fuck's wrong?" He went on cursing at me.

This is from a note that Catherine wrote to me afterwards: *"Not only did he run over there cursing, he got right in your face. You were smiling and saying, 'Get out of my face,' the second time still smiling, you said, 'Get out of my face.' The third time, you were not smiling, you said, 'Get out of my face,' like you meant it. He jumped off the platform, screaming, 'You are fired, you are fired.' You asked him, 'On what grounds?' 'Using profane language.'"*

No one else heard this profane language that he claimed to hear because I did not use any. But he did.

Later on, when Catherine told the story in court, she said, "The foreman didn't say anything to me. But he came around the corner yelling and cussing like a sailor at Sam."

Anyway, the next day, Sergeant 60 gave me a written warning because I didn't call him, put me on notice and said I'd be fired the next time I didn't call him when something went wrong.

Catherine was the one who picked up the glass first and handed it to me so I could put it in the machine. So if the glass ran out, it was her job to call him. And it was the set-up man's job to make sure there was glass. But he didn't say anything to either one of them.

Catherine even said, "He came back and apologized to me and said he was sorry he cussed, oh, he was trying to be nice!"

213

WHEN I CAME BACK from vacation, he put me on a job that had bad fumes. Usually, they didn't put anyone permanently on it, but he put me on it and said it was my permanent job. So I wrote down the name of the chemical, brought home a little sheet with the information on it so I could keep it. That chemical was really unhealthy to be around for very long. I took it to my doctor, and he gave me a note to get me off that job.

THERE WAS SOME Saturday overtime, but it was voluntary. Sergeant 60 ignored that voluntary, told me if I didn't come in to work, I'd be fired. So I worked it. If I hadn't come in and then got fired, a lot of workers might have thought, "He should have come to work. If he wanted his job, he should have come." They wouldn't see what Sergeant 60 was trying to do. With something like that, only a few people would see through it. Some of those who'd been through the same thing when they were fighting back could see what he was trying to do. Maybe a few others. But not everyone.

FINALLY, HE PUT ME ON A JOB with a new operation and new machinery. They hadn't got all the kinks out of it, and it was acting up. I put a piece of glass on the line and worked on it. I hit the button to make the line move, but it didn't move. I kept hitting the button, but the line wouldn't move. Sergeant 60 and Tom were down where the glass comes off the line, and I thought, "Oh, they have got it down, that's why the line won't move." Tom was the repairman. So I stepped back off the line and lit a cigarette.

All of a sudden Sergeant 60 jumped up, told Tom, "He's not here for long!" Sergeant 60 didn't even know what had happened. He came over, yelling at me, "Why the fuck you got it down, why didn't you call?"

Tom came over and asked me, "What's the matter?"

I said, "I don't know, I thought you all had it down."

So Tom moved the glass around a little bit and said, "Hit the button." Still nothing. He moved the glass again, "Hit it now." Then it moved.

There was an eye to trigger the operation, but it was too little. That was the problem. The set-up man had already told them they had an engineering problem: they should make that eye bigger so it would hit the glass. If the glass was off a little, the eye wouldn't hit it.

But Sergeant 60 called me over to the desk and wrote me up and suspended me. He said I had a problem and didn't tell him. He said I had been warned about this: if I had a problem with an operation I was to let him know or let the repairman know. It was bullshit and everyone in the department knew it, but he suspended me.

While I was off, Chrysler sent a notice through the mail, discharging me. When they discharge you, they are supposed to bring you into Labor Relations with your union representative, and you go through what happened together. They didn't do that. They just suspended me, and while I was off they fired me. The same week. So they were definitely trying to get me out of there. That was November of 1987.

Don went around and got people to sign a statement against this supervisor, how he'd been acting and how he treated me. Almost everyone who was working that day in the department signed that statement. And Don and Tom and Catherine and some others wrote out statements. One black guy wrote up a statement saying he signed up to go to another shift just to get away from him, because that's how bad Sergeant 60 treated black workers.

One worker in the department sent me a personal note that said: *"Everyone knows his goal was to fire you. They also know how he would try to provoke you to anger. The department is behind you except the few pets he has."*

Just two months after I was fired, Sergeant 60 came at

Don and gave him time off. He saw what Don was doing, organizing people against the speed-up and supporting me. Sergeant 60 really was trying to "clean up the department." They wanted to push that speed-up.

I WAS OFF ABOUT THREE MONTHS when a union rep called me, told me the company might bring me back, but they wanted to talk to me first. I went into Labor Relations. Two officials for the company were there. They both talked about my bad attitude. Then one of them threatened me and said that if they didn't bring me back at my age I wouldn't be able to get another job.

I let them talk for a long time, didn't say anything. Finally, I asked, "What about the supervisor back there? His attitude is not so great. What about the complaints I made about discrimination?"

One of them said, "We're not going to talk about any of that." The other one accused me of "intimidating" the supervisors!

I had to say something: "The way you all try to put it here, the criminal is the victim and the victim is the criminal."

That's when one of them got up, said he was opposed to ever bringing me back and walked out of the meeting.

The meeting was fake, a set-up, just like the incident they used to fire me. I was fired because the company was trying to force workers into accepting the contract we had voted down already. One of the company guys in that meeting said he wasn't in favor of bringing me back until the contract was ratified!

Three more months went by, and the International finally called me in. I went down to Solidarity House and talked to someone on the staff there. He told me, "We got Chrysler to put you back to work, and you get $2000 vacation money plus another $2000 on top of that."

But I had been off about six months. So I told him, "No.

I am not even supposed to be off. It is unjust that I am out in the street. Why do I have to lose all this money and I ain't supposed to be off? No."

"Well, it's all we can do."

It was another fake. If I went back like that, I would have had to sign something, accepting that I was at fault. No, I wasn't going to do that. It wasn't right. If I agreed to what they wanted me to sign, the next thing that happened, it would be easier for them to fire me permanently.

Twenty-Four
Out in the Street, but Still Active

ONCE AGAIN, I was out of the plant, from November 1987 to July 1989.

I'd been through it before. When it's like that, you know how to deal with it. I had family and friends that helped me out. And I got unemployment benefits. In May of 1988, the state unemployment office issued a redetermination that I was not guilty of misconduct. So I was entitled to full benefits, without any penalty. I had to appeal it to get it, but finally it came through. So I survived OK.

I was out of the plant, but I was still active with the workers.

THE BLUE CROSS STRIKE started in September 1987, and it was still going on when I was fired in November.

Blue Cross workers were the first in that period to make a big fight against concessions and win. A lot of workers were thinking then there was nothing they could do, and UAW leaders and a lot of other union heads told them that. But they did it, those Blue Cross workers. They went out on strike. And they won. It was a big event. It backed the companies up a little bit.

At that time, the majority of workers at Blue Cross were women, and a woman was the president of the union.

During that time period, auto workers were mad,

thinking that something should be done, that the union needed to change what it was doing. I talked to auto workers that were happy to see someone fighting. They were thinking we should have done that, too, instead of accepting the concessions with every contract. You could hear guys say it: "These women step up and fight, and we're going to accept what's going on?"

One day at work, just before I was fired from McGraw, this guy I knew talked to me about that strike. He had heard the bureaucrats talking against Sally Bier, the woman who led the strike, and he said to me, "She's something else, man, that woman at Blue Cross." He saw that the International union was attacking her and not supporting the Blue Cross workers. It was all in the news, the things they said against her. That McGraw worker said to me, "There's something wrong with them, because she sure enough is with us."

Sally Bier speaking to Blue Cross strike demonstration, 1987

At some point in that strike, the UAW International was trying to convince those women at Blue Cross that the company wouldn't back up, and that was it. They were trying to convince the Blue Cross workers to accept some big concessions. It was like auto. At their meetings, a regional director was trying to take over like he would run the strike. I was in the back at one of those meetings, and I saw him try to take the mike away from the Local president. She hung on to that mike and told him, "I've got something to say, and I'm going to say what I've got to say."

They had meetings other places too, and someone from the International would try to take over the meetings. Some of the Local officers went along with the International.

But those Blue Cross workers had a strike committee they elected, and they had enough militants to prevent the International from stopping their strike. I think that strike committee did something important to bring workers together. Those workers were saying, "It's our strike. If those other union officials are not with us, then let them go. We'll do it without them."

They had a big rally on Jefferson. Workers at some of the places may have responded when they saw that. They did a lot of stuff in downtown Detroit, marching different places, blocking deliveries from coming in the Blue Cross building, everything. Buses came by, blew their horns.

Demonstration during Blue Cross strike, 1987

The company didn't want that strike to spread. It could have spread because a lot of the Blue Cross workers had contact with the auto workers. It was mostly women working there. And the auto workers had family, wives, sisters, cousins working there. One time, we had some workers from McGraw and some from Ford come down to Blue Cross and walk with the picket line. We did that. That was saying something else too. Most of those workers who came with me hadn't ever done something like that before, coming down there to someone else's strike. They really liked it.

That strike was going on more than two months when I was fired. I had been going to their demonstrations and to their picket lines sometimes. But after I was fired, I was free to go down and be more active.

I went with some of the strikers to other Chrysler plants to talk about their strike: Mound Road Engine, Dodge Truck, Sterling Heights, the Stamping Plant on Nine Mile, and Jefferson too. I knew people at those plants. The strikers were going other places too. They had a leaflet to pass out. And I'd tell workers I knew, "We're all workers. If they've got a problem, we all got a problem."

The Blue Cross workers who went to those other plants, they enjoyed it. They saw that they were spreading their fight, getting support. When I was with them, I'd say to the Chrysler workers: "Let the company know you support these workers. That will send a message. Think what we could do if enough auto workers joined them."

Those Blue Cross workers were talking at the plant gates, saying, "We're Blue Cross workers, we're all UAW." It was sort of funny listening to those women. They would stand in front of an auto plant and say, "You are stronger than we are, we need your support." Maybe the auto workers could have been stronger, but those women were the ones fighting.

Some other Locals, Ford 600 and GM 160, I think—I

don't remember who else—had dinners to raise money for the strike, and I took people I knew to one of those dinners.

I didn't work at Blue Cross, so sometimes a worker would ask me why I was there with the strikers. I would say, "Some of us, we have friends and family that work at Blue Cross. We're all workers, we're part of the same family. When the family has a problem, that's our problem."

Blue Cross workers stayed out about three months. That was a long time, but they didn't cave in to Blue Cross. I know they got pretty big wage increases while auto wages were still frozen.

IT WAS EARLY 1988, and Chrysler said it wanted to sell Acustar. I was still out of the plant. Chrysler was talking about getting rid of all the parts plants, and the union said it was going to put McGraw on the list. But we backed them off for a little while.

Some reps and other workers from McGraw went to a meeting at the Local 212 hall. There were maybe a thousand people there. When someone spoke, saying it was time to junk the union's partnership with Chrysler, a lot of people clapped and cheered. Even Local leaders who had been pushing the partnership went along with that. One worker at the meeting asked who was ready to strike, and the whole meeting yelled in favor. But then International reps started talking about how to do it legally.

Some people yelled, "Forget that!"

So the International called for a demonstration at Chrysler headquarters in Highland Park. I forget how many people came out—it was a lot. It backed up traffic all around Chrysler's headquarters.

Yes, the union leaders had to do something, especially when the workers were pushing like that. If they don't do something in that situation, the workers will run ahead of them. So UAW leaders did their thing, dragged it out and let it die off. They made the Acustar workers think they were going to lead a fight, so they could step in front of it. But all the UAW was doing was going right along, letting Chrysler do what it set out to do with Acustar.

If we had been organized enough, maybe we could have stopped Chrysler from closing those plants and taking back things workers had fought for, pushing us backwards to the way it was before there was a fight. Some of us said, "It's not enough just to protest. We need to strike all of Chrysler." But there weren't enough of us then. We were more organized at McGraw, and we backed them off from changing a lot of work rules at McGraw. So they went for other plants, the smaller plants first, and they closed four of them right away.

THE WORKERS AGAINST CONCESSIONS election campaign was that same year. There were a lot of people involved in that, some from Blue Cross, some trade union militants who had been fighting against concessions, some rank and file workers, and people around the Spark.

I was still out of the plant then. So I did a lot of stuff while I was out, going different places, doing this and doing that.

We went different places to get signatures so we could get on the ballot. We went all over Detroit, up to Lansing and Flint and Pontiac, downriver south of Detroit, and to Ann Arbor and Ypsilanti. In six weeks, we got over 37,000 people to sign our petitions.

We had twenty-six candidates: nine auto workers, one postal worker, one grocery store worker, two Blue Cross workers, three hospital workers, one custodial worker, one landscape worker, one day care worker, one restaurant worker, two homemakers, four workers from small shops. These were really working people, and they were running for election as workers.

WORKERS AGAINST CONCESSIONS
PARTY

We are fed up with the attacks on working people. The employers have cut our wages and benefits, while they raise prices. They have closed plants and other workplaces. The threat of being without a job hangs over us all. For many young people, there are no jobs at all. Workers' neighborhoods are left to deteriorate without decent city services; schools are closed; unemployment compensation, workers compensation and welfare have all been restricted or cut back, while our taxes go up.

The working people are paying the price, so that the big corporations and the banks can get richer.

Things have gone too far. It is time for workers to draw the line. There are many people who feel this way. But up until now, we had no way to make ourselves heard. The two big parties both speak for the wealthy. No one speaks for the workers.

That is why we got together to run a slate of candidates in the November elections. Some of us were active in the Blue Cross strike last fall. Some of us helped organize opposition to the Ford or Chrysler contracts. We all want to see a line drawn against the cutbacks.

In 6 weeks, about 37,500 people in Michigan signed petitions to run WORKERS AGAINST CONCESSIONS in the November elections.

This is only the beginning. But it shows that thousands of working people are fed up with what has been happening, thousands who think we should stand up and speak for ourselves.

We can use this coming election to show just how many workers are determined that the attacks have got to stop. Of course, it is only our own struggles which will really change things. But after November, any group of workers who wants to fight will know that they don't have to stand alone. They will know that there are many thousands more workers who feel the same way they do.

We are daring to do what has not been done in this country for years -- we are running a slate of working class candidates in an election. Twenty six workers will appear on the WORKERS AGAINST CONCESSIONS slate. It's only a beginning, but those who run things in this country can be made to pay attention to beginnings like this.

Let us show that there is a new wind stirring among working people. Let us say it so that everyone will hear: CHANGES MUST BE MADE.

If you feel the same way, help make this campaign as strong as possible. Spread the word. Please get in touch if you want to help.

Write us at:
WORKERS AGAINST CONCESSIONS
P.O. BOX 11516
DETROIT MICHIGAN 48211
Or call: **(313) 961-7742**   (labor donated)

Paid for by The Workers' Against Concessions Party Committee, P.O. Box 11516, Detroit, MI 48211

Workers Against Concessions statement

WORKERS AGAINST CONCESSIONS
SLATE OF CANDIDATES
(Listed by office and present occupation)

U.S. SENATE...................SALLY BIER, clerical worker

STATE BOARD OF EDUCATION......ANNETTE JOHNSON, homemaker
                             and
                             VERNA BAIRD, homemaker

CONGRESSIONAL DISTRICT I (Detroit, Highland Park)
     U.S. Congress............SAM JOHNSON, autoworker
     State Representative
          District 1..........WILLIE D. WHITE, autoworker
          District 3..........MARCO F. CIOCCIO, grocery store worker
          District 9..........FRANCISCO P. SWARTZ, custodial worker
          District 10.........DONALD COOK, autoworker
     Wayne County Commissioner
          District 3..........RUTH EATON, custodial worker
          District 5..........MEGAN IRWIN, hospital worker

CONGRESSIONAL DISTRICT 2 (Ann Arbor, Jackson County etc.)
     State Representative
          District 40.........ROBERT E. CUNDIFF, auto parts worker
          District 53.........SCOTT JONES, restaurant worker

CONGRESSIONAL DISTRICT 6 (Pontiac to Lansing)
     U.S. Congress............JUDY CHRISTENSEN, printer
     State Representative
          District 20........ RICHARD CLAY PRINCE, machine operator

CONGRESSIONAL DISTRICT 7 (Flint)
     U.S. Congress............GARY WALKOWICZ, autoworker

CONGRESSIONAL DISTRICT 12 (Macomb County)
     U.S. Congress............VINCENT MARIO CONTRERA, tool and die

CONGRESSIONAL DISTRICT 13 (Detroit)
     U.S. Congress............MARTINEZ ALFRED GOMEZ, postal worker (retired)

CONGRESSIONAL DISTRICT 14 (Hamtramck, Detroit, East Detroit, Warren,
                          Sterling Hts, Hazel Park, Madison Hts. etc.)
     U.S. Congress............JAMES BREELAND, autoworker
     State Representative
          District 11........LARRY CHRISTENSEN, autoworker
          District 12........MARK HOPKINS, hospital worker
          District 66........MARY MEADE, interior landscape worker
          District 70........JOSEPH J. ROEHRIG, hospital worker

CONGRESSIONAL DISTRICT 15 (Ypsilanti and Western Wayne County)
     U.S. Congress............RONDA M. (REED) BELL, autoworker

CONGRESSIONAL DISTRICT 16 (Dearborn and Downriver)
     U.S. Congress............RUSSELL LEONE, tool and die
     State Representative
          District 28........LOLA HOFFHIENS, clerical worker
          District 31........HEATHER BLAKE SULLIVAN, day care worker

Workers Against Concessions candidates

Sally Bier was our main candidate, for U.S. Senate. She had just led the three-month Blue Cross strike.

Most workers today think that nothing can be done. The Blue Cross strike showed there is something that can be done if workers stand together and fight like those Blue Cross workers did. They forced Blue Cross to step back. There were only four thousand of them. "If there were a bigger force, hell, think what all of us could do!" That's what we said in the election campaign.

We tried to raise that, to say that workers didn't have to keep going backwards. We wanted to let people say with their vote that they were against giving up any more concessions. We tried to raise the awareness of working people.

I ran for Congress against John Conyers. Twenty-one years before, Conyers was the one who told those young people on 12th Street, "You have to stop this, get off the street." And those young people came right back at him, throwing things at him, telling him, "Uncle Tom, we don't need you now. Where was you when we needed you." The same old policy that he pushed in 1967 only got worse. And by 1988, workers could see it was really getting worse.

I was a worker, daring to run against Conyers. Politicians like Conyers had lots of money to run. I didn't. I wasn't worried about if I could win. We all just wanted to put those ideas out there, that working people need to resist and to have their own representatives.

I went to shops and markets and talked to people at those places. They'd tell us about things happening at their jobs or in their neighborhoods. We talked right with them, "We're all working people. You're going through different things. I feel the same way you feel about it."

The main thing I said in the markets and at the factory gates was: "The politicians are just running for office to get a job. We should think about it. We should have someone represent us who thinks like we think, someone who feels like we do, who's been through what we've been through. Someone who feels like we do, they'd go at our problems. But someone who does it just to have the position, uhn-uh, they won't do that. They want to get close to that capitalist class that created the problem."

That was the main issue. People nodded their heads to

agree with me on that. "Yeah, man, you're right." Maybe they didn't think it could happen, because people weren't ready. They didn't think people could come together. But a lot of people were happy to have someone talk to them the way we did.

Sam campaigning, Workers Against Concessions

227

On one of the leaflets, we said, "The two big parties both speak for the wealthy. No one speaks for the workers." On another one, we said, "We don't have to keep silent while the corporations and politicians ruin our lives. We can refuse to vote for the people who stood against us in Washington and Lansing."

We wanted working people to be heard. We told them, "We can use this election to stand up for ourselves. With our vote we can show that workers are against concessions."

We were all interviewed by different TV and radio programs or newspapers. Willie White and I were interviewed on a TV show, something called "Black Journal." Willie worked at Chrysler Jefferson.

We had a couple big billboards, too, one on the Chrysler Freeway, and one where the Lodge Freeway comes into downtown. There were a lot of smaller ones, but I don't remember where they were.

We were part of a parade going out Warren Avenue on the East Side. We had banners, some signs. My niece was a candidate, and two of her kids were walking there with us. We had a few people from Ford there. There were five Chrysler workers who were candidates.

We needed money to pay for the campaign. We asked people we knew to pledge a donation. We collected money at the plants, sold T-shirts and buttons that had our Workers Against Concessions sign on it. We had a cabaret. People organized card parties and yard sales for us. We wore those T-shirts when we were out campaigning so people could see us.

We had a big rally at St. Andrews Hall in downtown Detroit, a couple weeks before the election, and we all spoke. There were a few hundred people there. It was the first time I spoke politically to that big a crowd.

At least 30,000 people voted for the different candidates running on the Workers Against Concessions slate, maybe as many as 40,000. They were voting for a slate of candidates who spoke as workers, who were workers, and felt the way workers were feeling about their problems. Workers' candidates. It was about one per cent of the vote in the districts where we ran. That wasn't much. But it showed that a certain number of people at that time agreed with what we were saying, and they were ready to give us their vote.

Sam's niece Annette Johnson with two of her children during 1988 campaign

"MODERN OPERATING AGREEMENT"—that's the name UAW leaders gave to the local contract they tried to push on us in the summer of 1988. When it was voted down once, they brought it back for another vote. It was just a new version of the contract we turned down in 1987. Don Green and Erskine Terrell and some others put out leaflets about it and got people out to the meeting. I think Don and Erskine ran against each other for union office, but they agreed on this, vote it down. The second vote was a bigger NO vote than the first one, with seventy-nine per cent opposed.

In March of 1989, they brought the same contract back for a third vote. That time, they called it a "Competitive Operating Agreement." Different name, same shit. The company sent letters threatening to close the plant. The foremen went around talking it up. The International UAW sent a rep to the Local meeting to push it. He repeated Chrysler's threat that it could close the plant if we didn't vote for it. And they must have thought they were slick, because they put a provision into that contract saying that after the Local contract was ratified, I would be brought back.

I wasn't going along with it, and I said it: "It's a problem for me, being out, but we don't need to vote for that contract to bring me back. It's one more attack on all of us. We shouldn't vote to accept another attack. Vote it down. I'm not accepting another attack, and no one else should either. If we're strong enough, we don't have to go for that. They will keep taking things from us and making things worse for us until we do stand up for ourselves."

In the plant, almost everyone was against it. This time, it was voted down by an even bigger number, eighty-two per cent opposed.

What happened at McGraw was a little unusual. Workers there didn't fall for the threats. When workers from McGraw later went into the Truck Plant, they could see the difference. The McGraw workers stood up and didn't let themselves be bullied.

Twenty-Five
Back to Work and a Small Victory in Court

MY GRIEVANCE was still in the system, but the union and the company were dragging. The grievance just sat there. Finally, it went to arbitration in May of 1989, eighteen months after I was fired. That happens to people who are "problems," people who press the company or the union. Let them stay out there without any money. Scare them. In my case, they didn't take it to arbitration until after my lawyer Michael Pitt contacted the union and asked them for information about what they were doing.

Finally, they sent it to arbitration. The arbitrator ruled Chrysler had to put me back to work, but he didn't come up with back money. The union had all those statements and witnesses that my lawyer later used in court, but they didn't call most of them.

JULY 1989, I went back to work. I went back in there wearing my Workers Against Concessions shirt. I'd been out of the plant for twenty-one months, almost two years. Maybe Chrysler thought those months in the street would settle me down. No, if it ain't right, it ain't right. That's why I was fighting in the first place. If it isn't right, I am not going to stop, not going to settle down.

People around me made comments, "Glad to see you back." And I was glad to be back.

It couldn't have been more than a month, and Sergeant 60 tried to put me back out again because I had those T-shirts, Workers Against Concessions shirts. One day, something happened and the line was down and people took a break. Some of the workers told me they wanted one of those shirts. So I walked across the main aisle and gave this one guy a shirt. Sergeant 60 came up, said he was going to write me up for being out of my area. The line was down, the department wasn't working, and there were other people from my department out of the area. Three of them were outside the building. But Sergeant 60 said I couldn't walk across the aisleway.

The committeeman brought that up, "These other people are outside, you can't come back on him alone just because he walked across the aisleway."

But Sergeant 60 wrote me up anyway, said I was suspended for being out of the area. The other people were saying it was a set up because he didn't write them up.

I guess Chrysler didn't want to go through all that again. It was the same guy who did it before. It didn't hold up the last time, and it wasn't going to hold up this time. They probably said up in Labor Relations, "No, we aren't going through all that again." So they brought me back in a week, and eventually I got the money for the time I lost when I shouldn't have been off.

WORKERS IN ANOTHER department, not far from me, were mad at something. I had talked to them, to some of the younger workers, about what happened at Dodge Main when we went up in a big group to the superintendent's office. So some of them decided to go up there to the superintendent's office at McGraw. They came and told me, "We're going, you going with us?"

"Yeah, I'll go with y'all."

We got up there, people started talking. There were about

ten of them, all from the same district. Most of them were younger. They went up there on their own, no union rep. I don't remember any more exactly what it was about. It was something going on in their district they didn't like. Whatever it was, management backed off when they saw all those people go up there together. You know that those workers were surprised and happy when they saw management step back. Most of the time, they feel there's nothing they can do about it. But that time, they did something and the company backed off.

MY BACKPACK was gone. I had flyers in there, some books, a couple papers, things I wrote out from information workers gave me, a lot of stuff. I came back from the restroom and it was gone. This young guy training to be a supervisor, he had grabbed it up and took it and stashed it somewhere, didn't say anything to me. But the other workers told me he took it.

I asked him, "What did you do with my bag? Why did you move it?"

He said, "Well, your bag's supposed to be put up. It's not supposed to be lying around with tours coming in."

"How are you going to feel, you riding that little bike, if you park your bike and come back and it be gone?"

That guy went to the Snake and told him I said I was going to take his bike. The Snake was a general foreman or something like that then, not a regular foreman. It seemed like the Snake didn't want to have no part of it. He told the trainee supervisor to go talk to JW. I think JW was his number one supervisor. JW was well known, a black supervisor, respected by most workers. The Snake figured he could deal with it.

JW came up and told me the guy was worried I was going to take his bike.

"I ain't taken his bike. I didn't say I was gonna take his

233

bike. I just asked him how he would feel if it was gone."

He explained to the trainee that he had been knowing me for a long time, and he didn't think I would steal his bike. JW said, "Why don't you guys get together and shake hands and agree on it?" So we did. That was it.

JW wasn't stupid like some supervisors. He wasn't jumping up all nasty just to show how tough he was. Most of the time, we got along with him OK.

SOMEONE WAS collecting money to give the supervisor a gift at Christmas. I think it might have been the alternate steward. When he came over where I was, I raised it: "This supervisor makes more money than you, makes more money than the steward. If you want to give a gift, give it to the steward who represents you, not to the supervisor."

I told the others, "Here's this supervisor, you all are giving him a gift. He's OK with the workers most of the time. But he's the company. He's giving out the policy of the company."

Some people gave. Probably there would have been more if I hadn't spoken out against it.

That was JW, too. Later on, I told him, "It wasn't nothing personal. It's just what I see."

ONE DAY I was in the cafeteria. This guy from Labor Relations—he was a black guy—slid up to me and said, "Hey man, we can get along. I know you had problems. But we can get along. You do your job, and I'll try to do mine." So I knew they didn't want any more problems.

MY TRIAL against Chrysler started early in April, 1990. I was suing Chrysler for all the time I lost and for damages. My lawyer, Michael Pitt, filed charges two years before that. For more than a year, he interviewed my witnesses and the guy who fired me and some of Chrysler's witnesses.

And Chrysler's lawyers interviewed me and my witnesses. They'd schedule an interview, then Chrysler's lawyers would postpone it. So it dragged. I forget all the steps we went through, but it dragged.

Finally, we went to trial. It lasted about a week. Tom Sobczak and Don Green, they both testified. Both these guys were white, and had twenty-five years seniority both of them, and they were part of my defense in a case about racial discrimination. They testified about what happened in the incidents Chrysler used to fire me, and what the foreman had said, how he disciplined black workers worse than white workers, and how he treated me different.

Catherine Charles made a good impression on the jury too. She showed that I wasn't at fault for the glass missing in the first incident. She stated right off that she removed the glass, that it was her job to take the glass first, not mine, but he came at me. He did nothing against her, only against me. He wanted something to use against me, not her. She told the jury that. She was very quiet, but you could see the way she was on the stand that she was telling the truth.

Ron Brownlee, the young guy that Sergeant 60 stood over when he first got there, was a witness and he told how I stood up for him on the job, how I looked out for other workers.

They were some really good witnesses. They were right there, they saw what happened and they weren't afraid to tell the truth. And Chrysler's lawyers couldn't get them to back down.

Their testimony convinced the jury that there was prejudice against me. And we had other statements. Charles Hill gave a statement about the way black workers were treated. I think Jimbu filed a complaint too.

Chrysler brought in a black supervisor as a witness. He said he had problems with me too. Chrysler was trying to say, "It's not discrimination, there's no prejudice there, a black supervisor had a problem with Sam too." But when my lawyer questioned the two supervisors, they contradicted each other and they changed their own stories.

I was watching the jury, watching how they reacted when Chrysler's witnesses were up there. The jury seemed to be looking at each other, like they were saying, "What?" I could read that. They were thinking, "Something's wrong here."

Chrysler had a big-name law firm to represent them, and several lawyers took turns at the trial. All I had was my one lawyer, Mike Pitt and his legal assistant, Susan DeWinter, but they were good at it. Mike knew what happened in those plants. He knew what to ask, he could see through what Chrysler's witnesses said, and each time they contradicted themselves, he jumped on it. But I also had that support from the plant.

Chrysler's lawyers argued that the union did not defend me. And that was true. It shows what has happened to the unions. But I had workers on my side. And that came out in court.

The jury was nearly even, one or two more white than black, I forget exactly, and they were mostly workers. They knew, they'd seen it before, a company trying to get someone.

April 10, 1990, the jury ruled for me. When the jury came back and said they found in my favor, I felt better. It was something I had been going through for almost three years, and finally it was over. It was a big relief.

I went in the plant and told workers that the jury took my side against Chrysler. And the news went through the plant. Most of the workers were happy that Chrysler lost.

Three weeks later, I got a letter in the mail, saying the judge overruled the jury's verdict on May 1. We called Mike Pitt and asked him, "Can he do that?"

He told us that it can happen, but very rarely does a judge overrule a jury. But this judge did. He had been ruling against us all during the case. So that put the whole thing on hold once again. We had to start going through all the appeals. Before it was all over, it would take another four years.

The union officials who didn't defend me went around celebrating that the judge overruled the jury. A jury made up of workers took a worker's side, and some union officials took the company's side. No wonder our union is weak today!

LET'S STAND TOGETHER

Some people say I won't work with the company. Our union leaders work with the company today. That doesn't stop the company from attacking us. I say, we have to be organized -- so the company will understand it has to work with us.

Some people say I'll have you out on strike all the time. It's not me who can decide. It's the membership who should decide every important question facing us, especially on whether or not to strike. Today, we make decisions, but the local officers ignore them. I say, that must change.

Some people say they don't agree with my politics. All of us have different religious and political views outside of here. Isn't that our right in a democracy? The real question is what anyone will do who is elected to union office.

THIS IS WHAT I PROMISE TO DO:

-- I will give complete information to the membership. No secrets from the membership. No deals cut with the company.

-- I will tell you the truth about what we will have to do to get what we want, but I will never decide something for you. The membership will make the decisions.

-- I will stand beside any worker who wants to resist the company's attacks. No one under attack will stand alone.

-- I will fight against everything which divides us. No more discrimination or favoritism.

-- No union official, no matter how good, can do it alone. But I promise I will do everything I can to organize the membership and make the company respect us once again.

I WANT A UNION WHICH IS ORGANIZED. I WANT A UNION CONTROLLED BY THE MEMBERSHIP. I WANT A UNION 100% ON THE WORKERS SIDE.

This is what I think. If you agree, then give me your vote.

SAM JOHNSON
For PRODUCTION
COMMITTEEMAN
labor donated

Leaflet, 1990 election, McGraw

LOCAL ELECTIONS came right after the trial. I was running for committeeman, along with Larry McKinney, who was running for steward, and W.C. Williams, for the Executive Board.

Part of the time I should have been campaigning, I was in the courtroom or in the lawyer's office for my case against Chrysler.

A day or two before the election, the committeeman I was running against dumped a surprise leaflet in the plant, saying I owned two Japanese cars and just rented the Dodge Dynasty that I drove—like I rented it just for the election campaign.

"Sam doesn't buy American cars, he doesn't care for the workers' cause. People like him caused the job losses at Chrysler." That's what the committeeman was trying to say.

I said at the time that it was two lies and one slander. I'd owned a lot of cars. One of them had been a Honda. The Dynasty was mine.

But the real lie was what he said about job losses.

The contracts we had been fighting against were contracts that opened the door to more speed-up. That is what caused the biggest job loss. More production, fewer workers, the chase after more profit—that's what caused the job loss. Not the workers at Honda or Toyota or VW.

Jobs were lost at Chrysler when Chrysler outsourced parts jobs to low-wage parts plants in the U.S. There were still jobs, but wages were cut. And workers at those low-wage plants couldn't even buy a new car.

But a lot of workers believed those lies in those days. The big politicians were saying it, the union officials were saying it. And workers didn't see through that then. But it was a lie, and the lies have gotten much worse today.

Buying other cars doesn't cause job loss. Whether I bought a Chrysler car or a GM car or a Ford or a Honda, there were workers making those cars. Maybe they weren't all

UAW workers, but they were workers. And a big reason that all those workers at the Honda, Toyota and other Japanese plants in this country don't want the UAW is because UAW leaders attacked them all during those years. When the companies told those lies, they were trying to divide the workers, to pit worker against worker. When the union leaders did it, they were trying to excuse themselves for not leading a fight.

Those lies are company lies, pushed on us so the companies can make a bigger profit. They try to tell us they can't give us higher wages because they didn't sell enough cars. Other workers definitely aren't causing the problem. The companies are.

It's just like what some people say today against the immigrants, saying they're here and taking your job. How could someone come here and take your job? When the bosses get us to blame workers from another country, they get us to accept less. Those immigrants are not taking your jobs. It's the bosses' policy to pay them half and get rid of you. And no one is fighting against that. If the unions were fighting to push up wages everywhere, how could the companies use the immigrants against the rest of us? If we were all working at good wages, that would create more jobs, because we'd all be spending our wages, buying more things. It's the low wages that are taking jobs.

At Dodge Main, that same lie was in my mind too: the Arabs are coming in and taking our jobs. That's what I thought at first. But once I got the bigger picture, I realized that this wasn't what was happening. We had to be ready to fight for all the workers, not just blacks, not just American workers, but all the workers.

That's how rotten the bureaucracy was. Don't do nothing, push the speed-up, make sure the company gets the production it wants. That's what took the jobs.

Anyway, with all that, I didn't win that election. That

last leaflet just the day before the election hit like a bomb in the plant. I didn't have much time to answer the lies, and I was going against all the propaganda the unions had been feeding workers.

I RAN FOR DELEGATE to the UAW Convention in 1992, and that time I did win. I told workers, "Our union is in bad shape today, everyone says it. We need a new policy, and we need delegates who will go to the Convention to fight for this new policy.... We must make it clear to every company that the UAW will no longer give up concessions, nor will we give up jobs." And I talked again about the way they divide us, one plant against another, one company against another, one department against another, one worker against another. I raised that idea again: "They try to divide us, pitting white against black, men against women, skilled against the unskilled, American workers against foreign workers. And we lose."

It was a close race. The Local president Wilbur came in three votes behind me. I was just an alternate delegate, but the people decided to send me out to California.

The main thing about that convention was that Jerry Tucker ran against Owen Bieber for UAW president. I think that was the first time since right after World War II that someone challenged the bureaucracy that ran the union.

I thought the support for Tucker would be much stronger at that convention because workers were really fed up. Tucker had been organizing around the concessions. I went to St. Louis a few years earlier for a meeting when Tucker and others were trying to set up New Directions, and it seemed then like opposition was growing.

Some people did speak out at the convention. But the bureaucracy was running things, still controlling it. They made it hard for anyone supporting Tucker to speak from the floor, and they twisted arms to keep people from voting for him. Later on, I heard that a number of the people who promised to vote for him backed out at the last minute. To me that convention was almost like it was at the Local hall at Dodge Main. It was controlled. They used all those procedures to keep people from discussing any problem that came up—just like at the Dodge Main Local meeting, only much bigger. You could see that at the Convention, too. You saw people from here and from there, but most of them were either in cahoots to keep the bureaucracy going or they were afraid to stand up. Maybe they felt it wouldn't make any difference. People who are militants will say their piece anyway. But the others come, I guess, just for the party. They worry that if they do say anything, the International will screw their Local. But their Local gets screwed anyway by the union's policies.

Bob King organized a couple of buses from our Region, taking some of us just a couple of miles down into Mexico. Mexican union leaders met us, they spoke and King spoke. But we didn't get a chance to talk to any Mexican workers.

It was all a big show. The UAW was steady making propaganda against foreign workers, getting American workers to think other workers are "taking our jobs." But he pretended we were all standing together.

I got to see my daughter while I was out there for the Convention. Lulu brought her baby with her and her oldest sister brought one of hers, and they both drove down there to San Diego. I got them a room and they stayed for a day or two. So I got to see my granddaughter, T'Keyah, for the first time. She was only a few months old.

SO THEN IT WAS BACK to McGraw. One day, we'd all been talking. Someone said, "We're in prison here, just like behind bars." Don jumped up and hollered, "Hey man, I got an idea, we're gonna get some shirts printed." Don came up with the idea of that T-shirt with prison bars on it, the one that said, "McGraw Glass Sentence 30 Years." He got them printed up someplace. We wore them in the plant. Other workers wanted them. I forget how many he got printed, but I know McGraw workers bought a lot of them, maybe all he got. People were always wearing those shirts around the plant. I still have that shirt today, a couple of them. Years later, I was out at Dodge Truck, wearing my "McGraw Glass Sentence 30 Years" shirt, and a worker who came to Truck from McGraw stopped to tell me he still had his.

IN AUGUST 1993, my case was finally finished in the courts. We had appealed the judge's decision to the State Court of Appeals. The Appeals Court overruled the judge and put the jury's decision back. Then Chrysler appealed to the Michigan Supreme Court. The Supreme Court let the Appeals Court decision stand. That was close to six years from when I was fired. Chrysler finally had to pay me.

But even that dragged on. It wasn't until March 15, 1994 that everything was finally settled.

I got some flyers printed up, and went around the plant inviting people to a party. I told workers, "I finally got my money, come party with me at the Local," with the date and all that. I posted them, too. Somebody in management called me in and told me I couldn't be doing that, I couldn't be putting information out about the case

"Hell, I'm only just talking about my party, what's the problem?"

There was someone at the Local who catered parties, and they fixed up the food and drinks. Some people from the Local set up the room, helped lay out the food.

A lot of workers from McGraw came, workers who had supported me all that time, they all came to the party at the Local. I invited the lawyer and he and his wife came. Sally Bier was there with other people from her Local. And people from Spark who had helped me all through on the case were there.

People talked about how nice it was. I wanted to put out enough money to make it a nice party. There were a lot of people who supported me. And I wanted them to feel that they had a victory too, that it was the workers' victory.

After all those years, I could finally give some money to people close to me. There were a lot of people in my family who needed it. There's a lot of them. Sadie B., my mother, needed a new roof. I gave her money for that, so she didn't have to dip into her little bit of money. When my daughter came through, I could give her some money on a car. Someone had helped me have a car when I was off. I paid him back. Other people helped me out during all those months. I paid them back.

AFTER I WON THAT SUIT, people would come to me when they got a problem. They would be thinking that maybe if they had a lawyer they could get something. They wanted to know what was my lawyer's name, who was my lawyer. I gave them his name and told them, "You can contact him." But a lot of those people's cases, the way the law is written, there was nothing a lawyer could do. Most of the time, the way the law is written, you are screwed. And I tried to talk to them, trying to get them to see that they could deal with some of those things themselves.

It's true I had a good lawyer. But I also had support in the plant, and when I went to court, that counted, all those workers who supported me.

ONE DAY, TOM WAS TALKING about problems where his son worked. It was a little auto supply store. His son and other workers there were upset, but they couldn't see anything they could do, it was such a small workplace. I don't remember any more what it was about.

I told Tom, "We can go out there and support him. Not

just him, but the other people inside." Tom said, "Let's do it, keep people from going in." He really wanted to help his son out.

So one Saturday, we drove out there, Tom, Don and Don might have brought someone, and I talked to the guy who handed out the "Spark" newsletter at the McGraw gate, and he came and brought someone. A couple other workers from our department were there. Maybe a dozen people came out there, or a little more.

We had some signs, and we told the people who had come over there to shop what was going on, how that store treated its workers. We'd say to them, "If it had been your son, how would you feel about it? Do you think it's right?"

Most of them, they were working every day. They knew, something's wrong. If all those people are standing out in front with flyers, something's wrong. Everyone was real friendly. They knew what we were talking about. It was just like what they saw themselves. They were working people themselves.

When we talked to them and told them why we were out there, many workers turned around and went back. They knew that what was happening there wasn't right. They didn't shop there that day. The manager for that store was in the window, watching all that happen, watching people turn around. Some people went on in, but the majority turned around and went back.

After it was over, we all went over to Tom's house, and he had some stuff for us to eat and beer and pop. We sat around talking. His son was really surprised at what happened when we stood out in front, just talking to people, telling them how unfair that company was. He was really happy to see other workers interested.

Tom and his son were very happy to have people stand up against what had happened, to show that it wasn't just the boy's father. It was all these other workers from Chrysler plants that came out to support them, black and white.

MY DAUGHTER LULU came from Los Angeles in 1995 to visit in Detroit and brought her baby daughter, T'Keyah, and her niece with her. They stayed with Sally and me. That was only the second time I saw my granddaughter. Lulu wanted to get a car, so I got the employee discount and co-signed for her. I was trying to talk to Lulu about not paying too much for a car. I gave her some money toward it, but she was going to have to pay on it every month. And she was only working temporary then. But Lulu didn't want to hear that because she had in mind to get her an expensive car. I took her to a couple different dealers, trying to convince her to take something she could afford. But she had her mind set on—I forget what it was, but that was the car she wanted. I talked her out of it, and she wound up getting the Sebring. That was already enough, the Sebring. But when we got back, Lulu was still a little pissed off. She still wanted that other car. Her little girl hopped up and said, "We mad. We mad." T'Keyah was only three years old then, but she was a smart little girl.

Lulu said she was going to have a problem driving her new car back to L.A. She said she hadn't driven like that before, no more than two hundred miles at a stretch. And this was two thousand some miles back to L.A. Her niece who was with her didn't drive, and Lulu had a little girl with her to watch out for.

I told her, "You're strong, I know you can do it. Start thinking about it. Other people, women and men have done this. If they did it, knowing you, I know you can do it. You never did it. But that doesn't mean you can't do it." I talked to her about how to do it. "Break it down. Drive seven hundred and some miles and get a motel. See a motel where you want to stay, then get it, get rested, have breakfast there, then get out on the road, drive another seven hundred some miles.

Then you can do it." I gave her some money for the motels.

When she got back, she called. She said she stopped twice, but the last time, she had about twelve hundred miles to go, so instead of stopping she drove it all in. And saved the money for the last motel. She was happy with herself for doing that drive. Plus she had some money for herself.

ONE OF AUNTIE BEA'S twin sons was killed by the cops in Bessemer in 1996. His name was Calvin but we called him Twin. He was thirty-six when he was killed. The cops came looking for him, saying he had shot a cop's brother. They didn't take him in, they just killed him. Tried to say they had to shoot him because he had a gun. But they didn't find a gun on him or nearby. They shot him on the street, then he got in the alley and came into the house of a friend of his. There was a nine-year-old girl there. She said he was lying on the floor behind something. The cops just came in and started shooting him, shot him fourteen times, something like that, executed him. They could have killed the little girl. But none of the cops was charged.

The NAACP looked into the case, made a protest. Sally and I went down to visit my mother not long after Bea's son was killed, and we were part of a small demonstration about the killing at the Bessemer City Hall and then at the Jefferson County Courthouse. Bea was there, and a couple of my cousins. The lead guy who organized the demonstration was close to the family. He used to come by talking to my mother. And he talked to my Auntie Bea about her son being killed.

Sam, Sally and Aunt Bea in Bessemer protest, 1996

FROM 1997 TO 1999, I lost a lot of my close family.

In May 1997, my daughter Lulu died. She was pregnant, but in the tubes. When she first went to the hospital, they kept telling her it was just gas, and they sent her home. Her sister knew something was wrong when they went to see her. The hospital finally admitted there was a problem and stopped sending her home. But it was too late.

By the time Sally and I got out there, they had done surgery and she was just lying there. She wasn't communicating at all. We stayed in L.A. for a while. Then the doctors told us she was getting better, and she'd be OK. I got back home and went around to tell some of my relatives that she was getting better. I got back to the house, and some of her family called. She had passed. She was thirty-four years old when she died.

In August of 1997, my youngest brother Ocie died of cancer, probably from work. He worked at the Pontiac plant and at Dodge Main when he was in Detroit, and he worked in steel at Pipe Shop in Bessemer. And probably he died from drinking too much.

In July of 1998, Ocie's oldest son, Ossie Junior, died. He was in prison when he died. He lived with Sadie B. from the time he was a kid. When Grace came up to Detroit with the rest of the kids, he stayed with Ma'Dear. Ossie Junior was just a teenager when he went to prison the first time. The second time, he never came out. He'd been in there more than ten years when he died. That was just like another son dying for Sadie B. Ocie first, then Ossie Junior. He was just like her baby son.

In the summer of 1999, I went down to Alabama because Sadie B. was in the hospital. They operated on her throat for cancer. She couldn't talk after that.

She didn't ever smoke and didn't drink much at all. But there was so much smoking in her house, with all the people who came through, especially on the week-ends. Some years before, the doctor told her she had to keep the smoking out of her house. She put up signs, "No smoking in the house." So people went outside. Some fools would go in the other room and light up a cigarette, but somebody would tell them, "Didn't you see the sign, there's no smoking in the house." If her sister Bea was there, she'd definitely be on them about that. The other sisters came by too and watched out.

Once Sadie B. got home from the hospital, she couldn't do much. After the operation, she couldn't even talk. She was just lying down. Her oldest sister's daughters, Gracie and Hattie, came in and were taking care of her. A lot of people came to see her. A lot of people knew her, neighbors and others. Plus a lot of her family lived right there in Bessemer. Her sisters who lived near brought food over. Bea was there every day, bringing something over she fixed. Nephews and nieces came in to see her. Even the little kids from down the street, black and white, came in the house to see her.

Ma'Dear was the number one sister in that family. She wasn't the oldest, but she took care of everyone. The rest stayed with her when they came up to Bessemer.

That summer, I went down a few times. One day, I went in the room to talk to her. She was just lying there. She had that kind of sad look on her face. I was quite sure she'd been thinking that she was going to die, thinking about all the things she'd done in her life. I sat down and started talking to her.

I told her if she was worried about some of the things she did, worried that she might not go to heaven when she passed, she shouldn't be worried: "If anybody is going there, you will be one of them. All these people around, if they go, I know you will go. You should stop worrying about it. As many things as you did to help people. You looked after people. You looked after their kids. You'll go."

She couldn't say anything, but she kind of got a smile on her face when I said that.

That was the last time I saw her. She died in November.

The month before, October 1999, my oldest brother Willie died in Detroit. He had cancer of the throat, too. He always smoked and he drank a lot. After they found the cancer, he had this little thing in his throat that let him talk. It sounded kind of strange, not really like his voice, but you could understand him. He had that for about four or five years.

Twenty-Six
Retired from Chrysler, but Not from Militant Life

IN 1998, I HAD THIRTY YEARS at Chrysler. My thing had always been, I was coming out when I got my thirty years. Plus, I had decided after I got on my medication for high blood pressure that I wouldn't run in union elections any more. I knew I wasn't going to be able to deal with all the work on a day-to-day basis. I wasn't going to be able to do what needs to be done, plus work on a line at the same time. On January 1, 1999, I was officially retired. I was almost sixty years old.

THE COMPANY GAVE ME a clock and a retiree's badge and told me I was welcome to come in the plant anytime.

So I did that, I went back in the plant. I took computer classes the company and union set up for workers and retirees. I was still active in the plant, helping the ones left behind me to put out the "Spark" newsletter. I went from one end of the plant to the other, talking to workers I knew. If something was going on in their area, people would tell me about it. I'd go in with the newsletters, going from the north end, where the classes were, all the way to the south end. I'd see people I knew, give them a few leaflets, and they passed them on.

After a few months one of the supervisors told me I couldn't go into the plant.

"Are you saying I can't go to the restroom and the cafeteria like the other retirees do when we take classes?"

"Well, yeah, you can do that, but you can't go to other places in the plant."

That wasn't a problem. I would catch workers in the McGraw parking lot when they came in or see them in the cafeteria. They would give me things for the newsletter, and I would give them the "Spark" leaflets to take to others or sell them the "Spark" paper. Finally, I had a problem in the parking lot, giving out the workers newsletter and taking up a donation for it. Security said I couldn't do that. So then I met workers in a nearby gas station to give them leaflets for the plant and get their donations.

Just because I retired, I wasn't going to stop. I still wanted to bring the workers together, to keep them together. When I retired, I knew it was not over if I could still keep contact with the workers inside, and that's what I did at the plant with the newsletter.

We kept that newsletter going up until the plant closed, and the workers transferred to other plants.

RUMORS ABOUT THE PLANT closing got stronger in 2002. A top UAW vice president, Nate Gooden, made a statement: "Chrysler made a mistake getting into the glass business." The workers heard that statement and knew he was stabbing them in the back. He was going right along with the plan to junk the parts plants, telling Chrysler it didn't have to respect its promise not to close any plants. McGraw workers wanted to demonstrate down at Solidarity House. Our protest went on all day. About a quarter of the whole plant came out, and a number of Local reps. It was loud, I know that.

We had stood up at McGraw before, and some of the workers knew about the fights we'd made before. Some had been part of them. You have to look at that. They weren't ready to just lie down. That's what union should be about, standing together. Maybe most union leaders were backing away from a fight. But you still had some union people who were ready to fight, especially at McGraw. There were a certain number who were militants and fighters, and they brought people with them.

Some people say, "There's nothing you can do." But that's not how those workers at McGraw thought. They didn't just give up. Chrysler wanted to dump the parts plants, but those workers figured that if they fought, maybe they could back Chrysler up. And even if they couldn't win, they were going to fight. "We're gonna be out anyway, so let's do it." That's how they thought.

Two days later, the Local president stepped down. There was talk she was pressured by the International. And a few weeks later, two committeemen and three stewards were fired or suspended. They were all at the demonstration. The last of them wasn't brought back for almost a year. Some of those union leaders at McGraw were doing what needed to be done. That's why Chrysler and someone up in the International came after them.

MCGRAW OFFICIALLY closed in March of 2003. Some people were still in there working, but everyone was out of there by 2004. So Chrysler got out of the glass business.

Most of the laid-off McGraw workers went up to Chrysler's Truck Plant in Warren, so I went up there, helping pass out a workers newsletter when they were driving by there. Once or twice, someone I knew from McGraw stopped and got a "Spark" by the Truck Plant gate. Some of them were working up at the Stamping Plant.

I WENT ON SPEAKING at the Spark public meetings and the festivals.

The working population is being attacked all over the

country. Workers need to understand the attack, and why it is coming, and what can be done to stop it. Working people need the bigger picture, and you don't get that in the union, even when the union is fighting.

I know that people come to the Spark meetings to hear something different. I'd been around so many people. I could see where they were, and I wanted to speak to them. If you understand the problems, and you know where people are and what they understand about the system, you are trying to say something different so they can understand the system better.

DURING THESE YEARS, I went to a lot of different demonstrations and picket lines. Once you decide you are trying to pull workers together, organize something, you go because you get a bigger picture of what is happening by being at those demonstrations and strikes. If you want to see the working class move, then it's automatic, you want to be there to see what's happening, to see what the people who turn out are thinking.

IN 2007, THE UAW pushed through a contract that dumped retiree health care into what they called a VEBA, and it cut wages in half for everyone that Ford, GM and Chrysler would hire. This was the UAW's "Two-Tier" system. I went up with another Chrysler retiree Larry Christensen to the Truck Plant in Warren to talk to workers and pass out a leaflet against that contract. And we went to the Stamping Plant on Mound Road where we both knew people.

When we talked to workers at the gates, we'd say this: "We and you have worked all our lives, and they're trying to tear up the retirement they promised us. Don't approve this contract." And we'd talk about that Two-Tier. We'd say: "If you have family, a daughter or son or friend, the ones coming behind you, the companies want to push them backwards.

They should be further ahead than we are, not behind. Even if you aren't thinking about other people, at least think about your family."

The older workers were afraid of losing their medical care with the VEBA, but many of them didn't think there was anything that they could do. And some workers said, "Two-Tier, it's better than minimum wage." That's the lie union officials pushed.

Better than minimum wage? Yeah, maybe, but you can't live on it. We are being driven backwards. That's not better for the working class today.

There were militants in other auto plants who were trying to stop this contract. The vote was close at Chrysler. But it did pass.

Please hear what we say about this contract.

We, Sam Johnson and Larry Christensen, are former chief stewards at Chrysler.
Sam was steward at old Dodge Main, Local 3, and was a convention delegate at McGraw Glass, Local 227. He retired in 1999.
Larry was steward at Warren Truck, Local 140, Dept. 9170. He retired in 2002.

This contract slams the door in the face of our children and our grandchildren. They will never have what we had. All but a very few will be sentenced for life to $14 jobs, without real pensions, without health care in old age. All over the country this will happen. Since 1950, auto workers set the standard for the country. This contract breaks down the standard. This contract sentences workers' children to working poor for life.

Don't close the door on our children!

This contract closes the door on active workers' opportunities. The good jobs will be re-classified as "non-core." It says all future "non-core" openings will be filled by "entry-level" new hires paid $14. If so, then transfers from the line to these openings must be cancelled. What jobs will be "non-core?" The list includes sub-assembly, inspection, material, driving, any job where you do not put parts on the truck itself. At WTAP "sub-assembly" could mean the whole motor station, the axle line, the door line, fixture loaders for robot welders, in fact most of the metal shop. Will you know which jobs exactly? No. They want you to vote first. Then "within 120 days" someone from the International Union will come and tell the Local which jobs they have made "non-core." They have already made the whole new Marysville axle plant "non-core." $14.00. Plus this contract "exits" housekeeping, which means, outsourcing all janitor work. And it further collapses skilled trades classifications.

Don't close the door on your own chance to get off the line.

This contract closes the door on promises made to us retirees and to you, future retirees. This contract breaks the promise of fully paid health care insurance for life in retirement. It raises our charges on office calls, drugs, and yearly deductibles we have to pay – and future retirees will have to pay. It begins charging us retirees small monthly insurance premiums now, just to get their foot in the door for later. It starts up a VEBA health-care substitute plan which is much too underfunded, and loaded with company promises to pay in the future – which will be worthless any time Cerberus decides to flip Chrysler. They talk about 80 years. Ha! After January 1, 2012, the trustees of the VEBA are free to bill retirees and active workers extra monthly payments in any amount they say. The trustees are also free to cancel more services, and to raise charges for covered services. After January 1, 2012, we can be blindsided with large amounts of extra expense we never expected. For our whole working lives we were promised fully paid medical coverage if we – and you – earned our 30 years.

Don't close the door on retirees. Don't close the door on the retirements we and you have earned for ourselves. **Don't approve this contract!**

Sam Johnson
UAW Local 227, retired

Larry Christensen
UAW Local 140, retired

Union labor: ours!

Sam and Larry leaflet against two-tier & VEBA, 2007

IN 2010, LAKE ORION workers from GM called for a demonstration at Solidarity House. GM laid off those workers, then reopened the plant, saying that the whole plant was going to be Two-Tier. The International agreed with that. The only way Lake Orion workers could keep their wages was to transfer to other plants, and a lot of them were sent to Lordstown, Ohio—two hundred and some miles away. Workers had their family, their house, their kids in school in Michigan, but they had to move. If they wanted to stay at Lake Orion, where they'd worked, they'd be bumped down to Two-Tier wages.

There were workers from different places at that demonstration. I remember one man, a ninety-year-old man who had been in the Flint sit-down strike. He was standing out there on Jefferson, shaking his fist at the bureaucrats sitting inside Solidarity House, telling them, "Shame on you!"

New hires had been getting Two-Tier wages, but Lake Orion showed that the auto companies wanted everyone in that second tier. And if workers let the bosses keep going, they'll finally make everyone Two-Tier. Not just in auto. Everyone's wages are going down.

WHEN TWO-TIER first came in, a lot of auto workers believed what the bureaucrats said, that it was only for the new hires.

Even if that was true, it's wrong. It's your son, it's your daughter coming in, getting that much lower wage. If you had a decent wage, they should be going past where you are. You don't want to take them backwards. But that's what the unions' policies are doing, taking us all backwards.

What's happening today? The young people can't make enough. They try to buy a house and they can't. They get kicked out of an apartment, and they have to depend on their parents and their grandparents. So you're still caught in that same trap if you accept Two-Tier.

And what happens when they bump you down? That's what GM did to the Lake Orion workers and to all those workers in the former parts plants. How are you going to live on half the wages with all your bills? You can't live on that. How do you pay for your house? You won't have the money. You're still paying on the car, because you need that for transportation.

But a lot of the older workers went along with Two-Tier. And that's why so many younger workers think the older workers don't matter today: "That's them, man, that ain't us."

You definitely have got to stand up. If you don't stand up for other workers, why should they stand up for you?

The bosses are always creating divisions. And those divisions have gotten much worse over the last years. We're being pushed backwards. If we don't stand together, we won't have anything.

Part Four
A Fighter All My Life

Sam Johnson, 2012

Twenty-Seven
The Big Picture

"OH, YOU'RE STILL HERE FIGHTING?" That's what some people ask me when they see me out there.

I am still fighting. I keep at it because this capitalist society is rotten, and it's getting more rotten. It should have been pushed aside by revolution a long time ago.

It's going to take people coming together to push it aside. One person can't do that.

But I think I did something important. By me and other people being active, other workers did things they wouldn't have done otherwise. If no one is standing up, it gets much worse. When someone does stand up, it's always possible that other workers will decide to join them and fight.

I was active in the union all these years. That's where some workers are at. You can't just be bypassing them, and get them to see anything you want. You have to get them to do something. Then they begin to see what kind of force they have. And there were some fights. But the unions go along with all the rules and regulations of this system. And we can't stop there.

OUR FIGHT TODAY IS FOR JOBS. Already in the 1970s, the fight was over jobs. We were fighting against speed-up. That's about jobs. When they get you to do more work, they can get rid of other people. And that goes on year

261

after year. It doesn't take long, and they will have you doing two or three people's jobs. That's one of the reasons young workers can't even get a job today. Or if they do, they can't get enough money to raise a family.

It's the capitalists' policy: squeeze more work out of fewer workers, cut jobs. Profit first, profit before the workers' lives. We've been going backwards and backwards.

There's no way we should be catching hell. Why should we have to go through these things when it's our labor that created the wealth, billions and trillions of dollars of wealth?

THE SCHOOLS ARE PART OF THIS CLASS SOCIETY. They keep the divisions going between rich and poor, not just in one place, but throughout the whole society. There are good schools in this country. But they're mostly for the wealthy. They don't put up schools like that for the working people and their kids.

Today, the bosses' politicians are closing schools in the cities, getting rid of the teachers, packing more kids in the classroom.

They say they don't have the money. Why don't they have the money? They had it. We paid taxes. There's money, but the government took that money and gave it to the big companies and the banks. They don't use that money for the working people and their children. They don't use it for schools for workers' children.

WITHOUT JOBS, THERE WILL BE CRIME. These young people today can see there aren't going to be any jobs for them. That younger generation that doesn't have jobs and what they need to survive, they have to figure how to get money, and some of them turn to crime.

You see crime because this system is so rotten against the working class and the poor.

The young people out in the street, they're a lot harder

than young people used to be when I came up. They have to be, the way they come up. There's so many more now out in the streets with no hopes, no possibilities.

They are some real fighters, but who do they fight today? Each other and maybe workers who live near them. They are fighting against themselves and against their class. But when there is a fight, when the working class really gets moving, we have to bring these young people along with us. They could fight tomorrow along with the rest of their class. Today, they're just robbing other workers that have a few dollars. The problem is to go after the real robbers who put them in that condition.

EVER SINCE THE SECOND WORLD WAR, I knew war was a problem. Who are the wars for? They're not for working people. Working people are going to fight these wars for someone else, not for themselves. That's what we have to understand.

It's their war, the capitalist class's war, but they use us to go fight their wars. The U.S. ruling class uses us to control people in other countries, so they can steal from those countries, just like they steal from us. When we understand that, we'll say, "Damn. Let them go fight their war themselves!"

We don't need their war, and we don't have to fight for them. If there is a war going on, if we're going to fight, it should be a war against them, to stop them from attacking us or anyone in other countries. It should be a war to stop their wars.

We don't need their wars. Our fight, our war should be right here for what the workers decide they need.

THE RACISM I SEE TODAY doesn't look the same as what I grew up with. It's at a different level. But it's still there.

There ain't no jobs for black workers. In Detroit, in other cities, they moved the jobs out of the city. They moved them out where most black people don't live. And there's no transportation. Kids in the city can't get out and back if they get a job. And the schools in the city don't train the kids so they can get a job.

They don't say they don't hire blacks. But the way it's set up, black workers can't get hired. It's the whole capitalist system that is racist.

The cops may not be KKK today, although some might as well be. But they have gotten much worse the way they treat people. The situation in the streets is tougher. And the cops are tougher. And when you see a cop kill someone, they may say he shouldn't have done it, but the courts don't do anything to him. They say he was just doing his job. The cops kill a young black kid quicker than a young white kid, especially if the black kid speaks up. And a lot of them out there in the streets, they do speak up. So what if they go to jail, they're already in jail—that's how they feel. So they front off the cops. And sometimes the cops kill them. Or these young kids end up in prison, for what?

This monster of a capitalist system was born in slavery. Slavery may be over, but the racism it produced is not over. And the violence of this monster system against all working people is not over. We're all of us, the working people, being treated like slaves.

"THERE AIN'T NOTHING WE CAN DO." That's what some people say. They're just repeating that lie that's been pushed on them.

The government says it will fix the problems. It's a con game they've been running to make us wait.

We can see there's something wrong with that. The problems haven't been fixed, they've gotten worse. Government is not fixing the problems, not for us, because the policy of this government is to fix things for the wealthy upper class, that capitalist class.

The union leaders today come right behind the bosses and their government. They tell us to wait, to leave it up to them to fix things. But if we look at what they did, how they fixed things, we can see they didn't. They want to be "partners" with the bosses. They go along with them, accept the bosses' policy.

Religion is just another part of that same system, running that same game. The ministers tell people, "Don't take it upon yourselves, God will take care of things for you." That's just another way to tell us to wait. It's a game, lies that have been around for a long time. It was that way in slavery, it was that way before slavery. It's that way today.

The creator of our problems, the ruling class, set up the rules and the controls. Every ruling class has pushed that lie, that things will get better tomorrow.

If it was true that all we need to do is wait and someone else will deal with these problems for us, the problems of the earth would have been dealt with a long time ago. Waiting did not bring about the changes we need. It made the problems worse.

WE'VE LOST MOST OF THE WORKERS in the plants who had experience in the fights. The workers today never went through fights. They haven't seen that. Those of us who have been there have to reach out to the young generation, let them know how we got what we got. The older workers who came through the fights have to get to the younger ones, let them know what we did. But the younger generation has to become more active because you know the older generation will begin to slow down, and for some of us, the time is running out.

The workers in the 1930s and 1940s who went out on strike—they shut the plants and occupied them, they sent a message to the bosses: "You WILL give us what we want." It's the fight that made the changes. It was the workers who fought, not the politicians.

Workers today have to do the same thing, but this time workers have to take the plants over and not give them back. We have to take over and run these plants, run this city, run this country.

I SAW THE POWER we can have during the black rebellion. The black rebellion shut all those factories down. Black people on the street had enough force to shut this whole city down. That's why the bosses hired more blacks, even off the streets. They created more jobs. And they couldn't just bring blacks in. There also were a lot of poor whites out there without jobs. They had to create more jobs.

That's what the capitalists are taking away from us today, jobs, because there is no fight.

You can't just make a fight, get something and stop. We can see what happens when you stop, the bosses just take it right back to where it was or make it worse. When you see that, you know you can't stop, you have to take it further, so the bosses can't come back.

When we fight, we have to keep that fight getting bigger, keep it going. We can't stop part-way, like the fights of the 1930s and the 1960s and 1970s did before. Take that power out of the capitalists' hands. When you fight, if you leave them there, they'll come back. When you stop fighting, they begin to creep back.

We can't just think about this country. We've got to clean it all out, make it all right in one swoop, keep it going. Workers with a knowledge of history know not to stop part-way when the working class gets going.

SOME PEOPLE MAYBE CAN FIGHT, can defend themselves. I knew how to do that. But one person is not going to change anything about this system.

When the people being attacked, the working people come together, that's what's going to change it all. We're the force that can get rid of this system we are living in. We are the force that produces the wealth. No way we should be living the way we are today, some people unemployed, homeless, starving. We should be having what that upper layer has. We all should have a decent place to live, transportation, schools for our kids like the best ones today, good clothes. We did the work that produced all those things.

We can take back the wealth our labor produced. If anybody can do that, we should be able to do it. We use our labor to make this economy work. We can organize our forces to set up a new economy and make it run for us.

WHEN THE WORKING PEOPLE see things from a class point of view, they will do that.

Maybe all the workers don't see the bigger picture today, but if there's a certain number that do see it, then they can pull the others with them to fight for what we all need. If those few who have a bigger picture about where we fit in the system are active, they can lead the fights, bring the others with them.

THIS SYSTEM IS CONTROLLED by this one per cent minority, much less than one per cent, this capitalist class. Their system is organized in the interest of the few, against us. They seem powerful, too powerful, those people who run things.

But it's not true. The force they use to run this system, it's us. The force they use to protect their system, it's us. They use Us against Us.

With the forces that we have, we can change everything, get rid of the capitalists running this society, build our society in the interest of the working people. We can do that. When we bring our forces together, the capitalists don't have the means to overpower the working class.

The working class can take the power out of the capitalists' hands, we can build a new society that serves all the people, in this country and around the world.

The capitalist system is organized for profit. The workers could start to build their own society, organized to provide for everyone, and that could lead to a communist society.

We have been lied to. Workers need to know what this word "communist" means and what it's about. The capitalists don't want communism because there would be no place for their crimes and their robbery. We need to forget the lies the capitalists told us.

The first things workers would decide to do if they took over, they would provide what the population needs, but most don't have the means to have in this capitalist society. All that money going to the capitalists would stop. All that money wasted on profit would stop. All that money thrown away in speculation—use it for what the workers need. The things we've been wanting and not been able to have, we can have all of that and more. When the working class takes things out of the capitalists' hands, we will run the society for what everyone needs. Our children will go way past us; they will develop themselves and become so much more than we are. That's what communism means.

YOU CAN'T JUST LOOK AT YOUR OWN COUNTRY. If you look at what happened in Russia in 1917, you can see that. When those workers took power, every capitalist country attacked them. You can't make a revolution in just one country. If you do, the capitalists are going to come back like they did in Russia. They surrounded it. They blockaded it. They starved it.

The capitalists have connections in different countries around this world. The working class needs its own. Workers have to set up connections to workers in other countries. They are feeling the same way we are.

You see that sometimes with workers who come to this country. There are workers here from all over the world. Some of them came from countries where they were fighting. Their experience can help us.

I WAS ALWAYS A FIGHTER, I wasn't going to back down from a fight. I got that from my mother, from my family, from those around me, from what black people have been going through for centuries. So maybe I let some other people see that it's possible to fight.

But we have to know what we are fighting for, and if we are going to fight, who we are fighting against. It can't be us, fighting against each other. That's got to stop.

I had to get the bigger picture, and I got that from those who came before me, and they got it from the people before them, going all the way back to Trotsky and Lenin and Marx and a whole lot of other working class revolutionaries like them.

I tried to give that bigger picture to other people, I tried to let them see what the fight could be, what it had to be— working class revolution. I learned what had happened in Russia, where they had a revolution. I learned what happened in history when the workers built their own parties and fought to take power. And ever since I learned that, I worked with other people to build an organization so we could get to that point, so we will have a revolutionary workers party.

I want to see this monster system ripped out. I want to see power taken out of the capitalists' hands. I want to see the workers fight to organize their own power and set up an economy that can provide for everyone. That's why I have been active all these years, and why I continue to be active today.